Making Worlds

Making Worlds

One Hundred Contemporary Women Poets

Edited by

Myra Schneider   Dilys Wood

&

Gladys Mary Coles

Preface by Anne Stevenson

HEADLAND in association with SECOND LIGHT

H

HEADLAND

First published in 2003
by
HEADLAND PUBLICATIONS
38 York Avenue, West Kirby,
Wirral CH48 3JF

British Library Cataloguing in Publication Data.
A full CIP record for this book is available from the
British Library

ISBN: 1 9 02096 70 3

Printed in Great Britain by
L. Cocker Limited, 58 Berry Street, Liverpool L1 4JQ

HEADLAND acknowledges the financial
assistance of Arts Council England

Contents

Preface

Thirty years ago I would have agreed with my American mentor, Elizabeth Bishop. There is no such thing as women's poetry, she argued. Poetry is an art, and like music and painting it must resist gender politics - indeed every other kind of politics - and justify itself aesthetically by transforming personal experience into lasting and universal language. Part of me still holds to that point of view, yet in the final decades of the twentieth century poetry was caught up in a sea-change that just as vitally transformed women's conception of themselves. It became impossible not to acknowledge that more and more women were writing poetry, and that in much of this poetry individual experience was found to be shareable and nourishing - if not always as art, certainly as a distinctive form of writing. The title of this anthology accurately describes what happened: lacking a world in which they could confidently define or redefine themselves, yet challenged by the stringent demands of new roles, many intelligent, gifted women found words to 'make worlds' of their own.

This is not to imply, of course, that the women whose poetry is represented in *Making Worlds* ever ceased to live in their own time. If anything, these poems show that over the years their writers have become more aware of their history, more conscious of a shared responsibility towards past and present. It is precisely this responsibility, rather than a narrow gender-consciousness or a post-modern taste for experimentation, that gives the work included in this anthology its coherence. That emotional truths should be revealed, that reality should find work for the imagination, that confidentiality should replace convention and social disguise - these are the principles that, without exception, underlie this selection of women's poems.

It is by no means a comprehensive selection, nor does it claim to be. Some of Britain's best known women poets today are not represented, while the women who are - most of them familiar to poetry readers - for the most part have lived through the social and cultural upheavals of the twentieth century. For this reason, shadows are cast repeatedly over the text by World War II, the horrors of the holocaust and the privations of post-war Britain. Illness and death - not only of parents but of long-engrained habits of class and family life - are more persistent themes than love or childbirth. Yet love and birth are certainly here, and there is room, too, for meditation, for wit, for celebration, for irony and, of course, for anger. Anna Adams sets a high standard for the anthology in her opening poem 'The Self-Portrait', and the level of the work that follows, I am happy to say, remains clear and accessible. I could go on to praise individual poets and poems for several paragraphs. But here, instead, is the anthology itself with its rich offerings of approach, mood, form and narrative.

Anne Stevenson

Introduction

All the poets in this anthology are women living in the United Kingdom who write in English, though not always as a first language. Our overall aim is to reflect the rich vein of writing by women and to show their increasing contribution to poetry during the last twenty-five years of the Twentieth Century and into the Twenty-First. Also, the diversity of women's poetry, often underestimated, is demonstrated in *Making Worlds,* and its continuing and growing vitality. One hundred poets are included here, from the famous and established to those lesser-known - our focus during the selection process was on the poems rather than the names.

We have consciously tried to adjust what we feel is out of balance in the critical appreciation of poetry written by women - primarily a concentration on too few individuals and a failure to recognise the imaginative power, depth of thought and range of content in women's work.

In the literary context of the past and the near-past (the first half of the Twentieth Century), due to a male-dominated poetry establishment, relatively few women poets were published in major anthologies and journals. This resulted in a tendency towards low expectations by women poets and an inclination to follow influential models who had made important breakthroughs in both subject-matter and the use of language - Sylvia Plath and Ann Sexton, for example. These iconic poets have had too many imitators, usually lacking the verbal skills of the originals. In addition, this has led to women being associated with personal poems, sometimes given the tag 'confessional', which confuses one of the main issues. For women poets have shown exceptional honesty about the emotions, exploring them deeply and with universal relevance.

Even today, recognition tends to be given to only a few women poets who are hyped by the media - this not only fails to do justice to women's achievement in poetry but is damaging to a fuller understanding of its quality and the many areas that this work now explores. To help off-set this we decided to include in *Making Worlds* parts of long poems or sequences, selecting passages which stand by themselves but also indicate the scope of the whole work. We have equally endeavoured to select poems invested with searching thought, wide vision and intensity of language, and which handle complex or unusual subject matter with skill. Technical adeptness was an imperative, but our criteria also included empathy and authenticity of voice; and we looked for poems in a range of forms, styles and tones.

Inevitably there are inclusions and exclusions here that will puzzle some readers - as in any anthology. It needs to be pointed out that several of the poets whom we wanted to include declined because they didn't wish their poetry to be in an all-women anthology. Also, as editors, we undertook that all three of us must agree on each poem to be included.

The women poets whose work is gathered in these pages were nearly all born before 1960. One reason for this is the co-operation between the publisher and the Second Light Network (SLN), an organisation of women poets aged about forty or over which holds a rich data-base of women's writing around the country. This was one starting point - but by no means the only one - for identifying the work here.

We have aimed to bring together poetry by women in a new way. Some of the writers are very well-known, but perhaps not all aspects of their work are recognised. Others are writing ambitious poetry based on long honing of skills, but are appreciated only within fairly narrow circles. Some are lesser-known poets who, we believe, have considerable talent. Together their work builds a picture of contemporary women's poetry which we hope will enthuse and surprise our readers.

Myra Schneider, Dilys Wood, Gladys Mary Coles

Anna Adams

The Self Portrait

I thought to draw my living mask,
    with lines, or light and dark,
so propped a glass up on my desk
    and made a charcoal mark.

But in the ground below my room -
    deep in the shadow-well -
a narrow desert longed to bloom
    and so I left my cell

and softly, down the spiral stair,
    crept to a bolted door
and, stepping out into the air,
    proceeded to explore.

Laurels intensified the shade;
    I pruned and thinned, then found
green ferns, and planted more, I made
    small areas of ground

by prising up the trodden stones
    and digging deep; I fed
manure, dried blood and crumbled bones
    into the barren bed

then sought out flowers to make bright
    the semidarkness; most
were toxic as the aconite
    or pallid as a ghost,

but all took root and grew. Pale fire
    shone in the gloom; bile-green
proliferated; nightshade bore
    black phials of atropine.

The belladonna, that arrests,
  man's heart, grew tall and thrived,
and henbane, on forbidden lists
  of killers, I reprieved.

When I had climbed the secret stair
  and sat again, and drew,
my smiling likeness hinted where
  the true self-portrait grew.

Black-House Woman

I am, myself, the house that shelters them.
My nerves extend into this skirt of stone,
this shawl of thatch. These windows are my eyes.
I am a hollow room, enfolding men.

The peat fire is my heart. This hearth is warm
always, for them, but through the open door
sometimes shy happiness steals in to me.
The sun lays yellow carpets on the floor.

My children bring home hunger, men bring storm,
and I absorb in quiet the sea-bird's cry,
the breakers' roar, till in the sleeping room
oceans and mountains lie.

They leave no room for me in my own womb;
by them, and by their dreams, my lap is filled;
I spread my skirts to shield them, I am home,
content to be my one forgotten child.

Tortoiseshells Overwintering

In my bedroom ceiling's shadiest corner
  a dark encampment of inverted tents
is sitting out the tyranny of Winter.

Like Israelites that keep God's covenants
    in sober arks, or nomad Bedouins
who hide rich mats in fustian tenements,

they fold the magic carpets of their wings,
    concealing hieroglyphics of the meadow
clapped between tatter-bordered coverings.

As dingy as the withered nettlebed,
    as drab as marbled bibles, charred by fire,
or chips of bark or stone, they could be dead

but hang by wiry legs, as fine as hair,
    close-clustered near the plaster desert's edge
like a proscribed religious sect at prayer.

This bivouac preserves the Summer's page
    during eclipse of dandelions and daisies;
it bears pressed sparks of sun through this dark age:

one night between oasis and oasis.

At Mauthausen Camp

If there is a god, he will have to beg me for forgiveness
    (Graffiti at Mauthausen Camp)

To use such sufferings
as raw material
for art, is not permitted;
and yet I wish to add
a token, like those flowers
on the Italians' wall.
I wish the dead could know
that we know how they died,
that we might touch their hands.
No monument can do it,
no bronze, no rusting iron,
nor formalised barbed wire,
nor Berthold Brecht quotations.
Perhaps this crown of thorns

with name-tags speared on each
pitiless spike, says something.
These photographs of faces
when they had flesh on them
express that they were loved
and individual
but cannot bring them back.
Perhaps they haunt the stairs -
these steep and broken stairs
that sweep down to the quarry
like a dry waterfall
that was a fall of men:
but they cannot return
to vulnerable sense
to be abused again,
and would not if they could.
I see the species-rich
meadow above mass graves
where Yugoslavs and Poles,
Hungarians and Jews,
Bulgarians and Danes,
Dutchmen and Frenchmen lie
by Germans and Italians.
I think: The Earth forgives.
Forgiveness is not just.
There can be no amends
except remembering
bloodfalls where starved men fell
beneath heartbreaking stones
and each was I - and I -
and I -

Fleur Adcock

Script

'Wet the tea, Jinny, the men are back:
I can hear them out there, talking, with the horses',
my mother's grandmother said. They both heard it,
she and her daughter - the wagon bumpily halted,
a rattle of harness, two familiar voices
in sentences to be identified later
and quoted endlessly. But the tea was cold
when the men came in. They'd been six miles away,
pausing to rest on Manurewa Hill
in a grove of trees - whence 'Fetch the nosebags, Dickie'
came clearly over. A freak wind, maybe:
soundwaves carrying, their words lifted up
and dropped on Drury. Eighty years ago,
long before the wireless was invented,
Grandma told us. It made a good story
baffling. But then, so was the real thing -
radio.
        My father understood it.
Out on the bush farm at Te Rau a Moa
as a teenager he patiently constructed
little fiddly devices, sat for hours
every day adjusting a cat's whisker,
filtering morse through headphones. Later came
loudspeakers, and the whole family could gather
to hear the creaky music of IYA.
So my father's people were technicians, is that it?
And my mother's were communicators, yes? -
Who worked as a barber in the evenings
for the talking's sake? Who became a teacher -
and who was in love with tractors? No prizes.
Don't classify. Leave the air-waves open.

We each extract what we most need. My sons
rig out their rooms with stereo equipment.
I walk dozily through the house
in the mornings with a neat black box,
audible newspaper, timekeeper and -saver,
sufficient for days like that.

On days like this
I sit in my own high borrowed grove
and let the leafy air clear my mind
for reception. The slow pigeon-flight,
the scraped-wire pipping of some bird,
the loamy scent, offer themselves to me
as little presents, part of an exchange
to be continued and continually
(is this a rondo? that professor asked)
perpetuated. It is not like music,
though the effects can strike as music does:
it is more like agriculture, a nourishing
of the growth-mechanisms, a taking-in
of food for what will flower and seed and sprout.

On a path in the wood two white-haired women
are marching arm in arm, singing a hymn.
A girl stops me to ask where I bought my sandals.
I say 'In Italy, I think' and we laugh.
I am astonished several times a day.
When I get home I shall make tea or coffee
for whoever is there, talk and listen to talk,
share food and living-space. There will always
be time to reassemble the frail components
of this afternoon, to winnow the scattered sounds
dropped into my range, and rescue from them
a seed-hoard for transmission. There will be
always the taking-in and the sending-out.

Kilpeck

We are dried and brittle this morning,
fragile with continence, quiet.
You have brought me to see a church.
I stare at a Norman arch in red sandstone
carved like a Mayan temple-gate;
at serpents writhing up the doorposts
and squat saints with South-American features

who stare back over our heads
from a panel of beasts and fishes.
The gargoyles jutting from under the eaves
are the colour of newborn children.

Last night you asked me
if poetry was the most important thing.

We walk on around the building
craning our heads back to look up
at lions, griffins, fat-faced bears.
The Victorians broke some of these figures
as being too obscene for a church;
but they missed the Whore of Kilpeck.
She leans out under the roof
holding her pink stony cleft agape
with her ancient little hands.
There was always witchcraft here, you say.

The sheep-track up to the fragments
of castle-wall is fringed with bright bushes.
We clamber awkwardly, separate.
Hawthorn and dog-rose offer hips and haws,
orange and crimson capsules, pretending
harvest. I taste a blackberry.
The soil here is coloured like brick-dust,
like the warm sandstone. A fruitful county.
We regard it uneasily.

There is little left to say
after all the talk we had last night
instead of going to bed -
fearful for our originality,
avoiding the sweet obvious act
as if it were the only kind of indulgence.

Silly perhaps.
        We have our reward.
We are languorous now, heavy

with whatever we were conserving,
carrying each a delicate burden
of choices made or about to be made.
Words whisper hopefully in our heads.

Slithering down the track we hold hands
to keep a necessary balance.
The gargoyles extend their feral faces,
rosy, less lined than ours.
We are wearing out our identities.

Letter from Highgate Wood

Your 'wedge of stubborn particles':

that silver birch, thin as a bent flagpole,
drives up through elm and oak and hornbeam
to sky-level, catching the late sunlight.

There's woodsmoke, a stack of cut billets
from some thick trunk they've had to hack;
and of course a replacement programme under way -
saplings fenced off against marauders.

'We have seasons' your poem says;
and your letter tells me the black invader
has moved into the lymph; is not defeated.

'He's lucky to be still around' said your friend -
himself still around, still travelling
after a near-axing as severe,
it yet may prove, as yours at present.

I have come here to think, not for comfort;
to confront these matters, to imagine
the proliferating ungentle cells.

But the place won't let me be fearful;
the green things work their usual trick -
'Choose life' - and I remember instead
our own most verdant season.

My dear, after more than a dozen years
light sings in the leaves of it still.

Gillian Allnutt

The Garden in Esh Winning

Go then into the unfabricated dark
With your four bare crooked tines, fork,
And get my grandmother out of that muddle of dock and dandelion
    root
And put an end to neglect
While the wind says only *Esh Esh*
In the late apple blossom, in the ash
And all the hills rush down to Durham
Where the petulant prince bishops dream
In purple vaults.
It's not the earth's fault,
Fork, but mine, that I for forty years of days and nights invented
    dragons
To guard my grandmother's bare arthritic bones
From my own finding. Now of all things I imagine a garden
Laid over, and dumb as, a disused coalmine.
In the north there are no salley gardens, no, nor bits of willow pattern
Plate to plead for me, no, only bones
Unmourned, the memory of the memory of a plane shot down
And its discolouration.
Who now humbly brings me my grandmother in pieces
Like Osiris,
Fork? Who eases out old sorrel gone to seed, old scallions?
Who pulls the purple columbines
Out of the not quite dark midsummer midnight? In the north the
    sky is green,
The long grass, partly shorn, lies down like a lion
And *something's happened to John*
And in this valley of discoloured bones
Ezekiel lies open to the wind, the fork-work done.
The Bible propped like an elbow on the ironing-board within
The house is full of visions, Gran,
Of what we are, were, always might have been.

*My grandmother's son John was an RAF navigator, shot down over France in 1943.
The night it happened, she woke and sat up in bed saying 'Something's happened to
John.'*

What You Need to Know for Praying

You need to know that no one has been here before,
not even you, though you are as ever

kneeling on the oblong Indian rug, its faded
tree, its dry blue birds.

You may imagine that
they sing. You need to know that

everyone who was or is or will be's
here with you in your always

unswept room. You may imagine it's an ark, the first or last,
and that the earth spins, scattering dust.

You need to know your heart
will beat

its wings,
will not berate you for imagining

you've sent it out,
a solitary raven, on its way from Ararat.

from: **Nantucket and the Angel: Sketches**

Gone

He's risen like the skylark from its nest of grass.
He's risen from his antic nest of illness
Awkwardly. For Gabriel has lost the knack and snare of wing,
Has risen therefore less as skylark than as man and in his going
Without gruel or grace goes to the graceful places of his own desire.
He's gone to lend the wind an ear
At dry stone walls.
He's gone to let the unattended school of hills -
The humpbacked whale and shale and vellum of them -
Sail upon him

Sitting still. He's gone to learn from lichen
Something of the scale and making of the skin.
He's gone beyond the field barn to the brown bogwater and the tarn
To sodden his shoes, to break his feet in, gone
To let the quibble of the sheep, the quiet of sheep-
Fold open sleep
In him. And well beyond the stone smallholding
He is gone, to let the affable unfolding -
Fell by fell and tale by tale, untold, star-holding - tell
Upon him and the yellow tormentil.

Moniza Alvi

The Twins

And so the twins were born -
not two infants
but a mother and a father.

Clearly they were not identical,
and they were not inseparable.
But suddenly they shared a birth-time
though they couldn't tell
whether they were years old
or just a second old.

Often their child filled entirely
their watchful compound eye.

Their hands were continually busy
making a sinewy cat's cradle.
At times their fingers moved
in sympathy as if one pair of hands
was sketching the other.

And these twins tried to wear
the same clothes - flecked
with their shaky authority.

In their darkest hours
they were afraid of falling
through the galaxy,
of snapping apart
at their shiny hinge.

They were two moons
two suns
two trees
bending over a hammock.
They were lighter, heavier
than they'd ever been,
more hollow and more solid.

And still their single lives continued
like the remnants of a festival
in another town.

And If

If you could choose a country
to belong to -
perhaps you had one
snatched away,
once offered to you
like a legend
in a basket covered with a cloth -

and if the sun were a simple flare,
the streets beating out
the streets, and your breath
lost on the road
with the Yadavs, herding cattle,
then you could rest, absorb
it all in the cool of the hills,

but still you might peel back one face
to retrieve another
and another, down to the face that is,
unbearable, so clear,
so complex, hinting at nations,
castes and sub-castes
and you would touch it once -

and if this Eastern track were
a gusty English lane
where rain makes mirrors
in the holes,
a rat lies lifeless, sodden
as an old floorcloth,
you'd be untouchable - as one
defined by someone else -

one who cleans the toilets,
burns the dead.

R.V. Bailey

The Greyhound

The Commercial took itself seriously.
Reserved for travellers; had a carpet,
A three-piece suite on whose uncut moquette
George and Daisy conducted their decorous courtship
When he had a few hours' leave.

Room for larks in the Taproom.
It had a piano, lent itself
To whoopee with the soldiers there. The fire,
Coaxed behind newspaper, roared at the draught,
Joining in the fun.

I never knew where the Smokeroom got its name,
Except it was a grey and gloomy place, long as a Craven A.
The fire sulked, always ready to go out.
Morose old men pushed dominoes around.

Time, my bonny lads, time my uncle cried at ten,
Over the bar, loud enough to carry
To all the other rooms, to draw to a close
The farmers' complaints about hay, the Hitler jokes,
The *Siegfried Line* in the Taproom. Time
For the bonny lads to travel out to the cold
Up the dark street, to the dark camp on the fell,
To the darkened trains, to wherever they were going,
Pushed around in the smoke like the old mens' dominoes.

Jill Bamber

Windmill

Sightless, he needed me to find
the working parts, ensnared my eyes.
I knew this jig-saw giant was beyond me,
wanted to leave the wind's geometry
and read the guide-book later, out aloud.

Putting his hands on cog wheels big
as barrels he pursued the twist of wind
from sails to millstone. We disturbed
the dust. A smell of creosote clung
to our fingers. We took longer,
letting people pass, part of the spectacle.

We climbed from floor to floor
on open stairs, hands on ropes,
rooms diminishing in size like rings
constricting, crossed splintered boards
and split diameters in black tarred walls
that seemed to drink the light.

The seventh floor was best. I caught
a sliding glimpse of sky and waterways,
a beat of white shuttering the windows
dealt like a pack of cards that never falls.
He lost me then, struck dumb, some things
unshareable, the pain a turning cross.

Hearing the creak of sails
he reclaimed me. The upright shaft
was turning with slow power. I saw
the fantail like a shuttlecock, light
as a child's toy against the blue
inching the sails foursquare to the wind,
both of us knowing, by the end of it,
we could have made it work.

Wendy Bardsley

October Apples

for DM

Only I know the thin scrape of her elbow
beneath my skin,
the nervous flicker of her fingers.
She is here now,
by me in this cot.
I do not even know
the colour of her eyes;
they are tight shut in a vow of silence,
snug in the hold of her death.
The red bell of her heart is stopped,
the little rivers of her veins have stayed their flow.

You have brought the apples in, you say.
The worms are soundless; teeth that gnaw
inside the great dumb mouth of fate.
I have pushed her out cold dead.
An odd gift for the sun.
Tonight you will come
and hold her,
while we cry.

Maya Ceramic Figure

From Campeche, Mexico (II ins)

If you sit squat, facing her, it might happen -
the soft pat of her feet,
the click of her fingers in the dance.

Her torso is smooth as sun.
Steady leaves of fingers have passed through
centuries across her limbs. She is saturated with love.

What tool has sparked those eyes?
The dome of her body is vast with antiquity
stretching a straight line eye to eye with me.

It is her Golden Age, wet with the echoes of water,
dry with silent time.
She is stopped as a surprised arachnid, her dance stayed,
a Coppelia in her maker's mind -
he might have had her *this*, or *this*...

She started when the wet heat bundled into stone,
clinging like the bony weight of bats, an each to each.

We are unable to decipher her pictographs.
Her secrets are safe.
But if I listen hard, she tells me *he* is here,
coursing through her fiery heart,
lacing the necks of hills with mountains,
holding the writhing trees against the wind.
Her left arm reaches out for him in a sigh of sand.

Pebbles

And shall I take a simple shape at last,
like these pale sisters, silent, still,
regardless of the bluster of my sea, my hurricane.
Poised jewels, beautiful and smooth and cool.
Who can break through to their mystery
and find the passion breathing
in the wild woods of their meek design.
They are the fury and the rage of the beginning,
blazing at the back of Time.
I am a tendril, naked with desire, searching a hold,
invoking *joie de vivre*
from the thin crack of the light. A gust today,
tomorrow sea-spray on the strange uncharted shore,
or something more I do not know of yet,
although I think I knew of it before.

Wanda Barford

Beetroot

Often, peeling beetroot, I think of you
my old young cousins, and I see your sunken eyes
and those numbers tattooed deep
into your fleshless arms.

Looking down at my stained fingers
I see your rouged cheeks faking health,
turned up to the guards, to plead
they postpone death a while.

The ruse worked for you; but for others
whose cheeks you painted - drained mothers
with pale children - it failed. They shuffled
into the gas-chambers wearing this loud disguise.

Elizabeth Bartlett

Lamb

Scrubbing the kitchen table
after the doctor has gone,
the pink of diluted blood
and carbolic soap swirling
in the zinc bucket, her child
lying listlessly sucking a torn
membrane of worn sheeting,
dampened with tap water,
she feeds the red-eyed stove.

Now she sets the table,
sharpens the knives, spoons
fat over the lamb's leg, throws
the aftermath of surgery
down the outside drain. Her child,
sick with tears and silent
sees Abraham in a white apron;
flesh squeals and shrinks
on burning railway sleepers.

Afterwards, she clears the table,
saves the red gravy for the baby,
makes a nest on the shiny sofa,
tucking round a thin grey blanket;
her child sleeps, daubed and stained.
Steeping night-gowns in cold water
she places bread upon the altar,
covers all with a cloth, crosses herself,
darns socks over a wooden mushroom.

A Nodal Point

I wasted my life on this:
it was friend, family, lover.
When rejection came it was
on a slip of white paper.
Acceptance arrived similarly,
signed Ed, promised a fee,
brightened the day unexpectedly.

My heart was held tight
in a clamp, a vice; my anger
burned with a fierce white light;
all my life was exposed on paper
and never lived, except haltingly.
Now, at the nodal point, I see
urgent buds on a dying tree.

I have come so far to find
the shadow of my father's hand
making rabbit's ears on the blind
for a frightened child, and
see him looking kindly upon me.
That I once loved unreservedly
is now clear, at last, to me.

The Beautiful Knees of the Visiting Lay Preacher

They say he is a charismatic teacher,
but I am only here to see
the rounded knees of the visiting lay preacher.

There are no candles or incense here;
he wears blue shorts and not a cassock.
When he prays, it's not on his knees,
or does he use a velvet hassock?

This plain chapel is the oldest church in town,
but gone Pentecostal, uses the gift of tongues,
tends the few remaining grassy mounds.

Electric guitars fracture the dead air,
there is healing and the clapping of hands,
trainers and T-shirts are statutory wear,
hymns have the beat of outmoded rock bands.

This is the way I am, you see.
Sometimes it's United Reform,
and sometimes R.C.
I've learned the protective mantra,
the art of meditating, gone Quaker
to see how it feels.
The Methodist handshake is sweaty
and cold, the pine pews gleam yellow,
the club badge is almost visible,
the congregation risible.

Spiritualists leave me cold.
Maybe it's a goose going over my grave,
or no central heating. The chilly nave
of high Anglican has the appeal
of a supermarket deep-freeze, the red fire
of vestments warming only
the faithful with their blue-rinsed hair
waiting for the funeral pyre.

How beautiful are the knees
of the visiting lay preacher.
How beautiful his spotless trainers.
Lord, forgive me please
for prayers like these.

I came here to be healed
by such visions of rounded flesh.
They enter the blandness of my days
like the slick lightning flash
upon the landscape of my parched
and frightened soul.

Irish Hair

Coming over from Ireland, the boat
lurching its way in snapping wind,
the decks wet and slippery with spume,
the girl, Christiana Breary,
is leaving behind the stench
of rotting potatoes, the abandoned
household goods, the shallow trench
where they left her brother
wrapped hastily in straw,
the baby dead of road fever,
seeming at the last to cry
bread or blood, and then silence.

She is nearly six years old.
When she was four it was
a fine hot summer until August
rain and biting sleet
wetted her bare feet.
She does not know that the boat
will dock at Liverpool and not Quebec,
that they will throw her mother
into the sea, free from the misty confusion
of typhus, free from the unfounded illusion
of a better life. She does not know
that she will marry into pure Norman stock,
a man gaunt as a gibbet, melancholy
as an undertaker, and that from her
will be extracted a life of labour,
but not the smell of famine or abandoning
of home and children.

They brought with them the two
brass candlesticks, wrapped
in a camisole and a pair of corsets,
the youngest riding on his shoulder.
Her father will find a new wife,
now scrubbing steps in Watling Street,
the roads the Romans made, as he
will make English roads with his pick.

She is tired of serving the gentry,
but not crying of hunger,
the basement kitchen warmed
by well-stoked ovens.

Buying my bag of potatoes I hurry
to the hairdressers. Cutting
my coarse hair the girl says:
'We call this Irish hair',
and nearly a century later I now
think of her, Christiana Breary,
my father's mother, who made
her own pilgrim's progress
to an alien land, her bible in her hand,
and in her body her unseen corn seed
which will never exorcise the devil
of hunger, or my own anger.

Jacqueline Bartlett

Mummies

Each year
my grandad
slaughtered pigs

and hung the hams
and flitches
from the kitchen rafters
above the oak fuelled range.

He sat content
through the fugs of slow curings
while his skin
took on the colour of areca nuts
or old Virginia.

His breeches, boots
and shirt
hardened to a carapace
his mouth
became the drawstring opening
in the purse of his face

his hands
turned to leather, the veins
slowly pumping brine and ice water

and mahogany juices
gathered
beneath his fingernails.

He spent an age
slowly drying in silence

like the Inuit woman and her child
hacked from the permafrost
after six hundred years.

Jane Beeson

Star-eyed Fool

I lived as a star-eyed fool loving you:
thistles smashed as you swung round the field
in your old blue beat-up tractor;
I had to run ahead of you
to get the white ducks out of the Yellow-rattle.
When you came back for a fill of diesel
the tractor juddered like a live thing,
a horse over-ridden: it shook and shook,
fumes from the exhaust smudged the tree leaves
into undulating water weed,
even the gate lecks pulsed like idle fish.
I followed the geometric print of the wheels
over hot tarmac into the fields,
sank into the moist refuge of bank
my feet in white clover singing with bees.

Arthritis

What's the good
if I can't walk, can't stride
across the fields to see the sky
pinken like a white sheet
put in the washer with a red dress -
see the barn's shape blacken
gold-rimmed as the sun goes?

I am drawn out of the house,
magnetised to the last of the light -
a sunflower turning face
dreading light's loss,
needing rain, afraid to ask change
or interfere with holy order.

On this rock I stare
over the moor's cathedral -
the long unmoving ripple of shapes

arching sensuous as the mound
of a working man's back. Hameldown
slithers into Kingsbarrow,
Kes Tor's hump jars,
Corsands elongates
to Fir and Yes.

O great hills I should beware of you:
the light grows luminous behind you
communion leaves you impervious -
no longer can I kneel.

Anne Beresford

What Do You Do All Day While I'm at School?

For Leah, my grand-daughter

Did you expect me to list
the potatoes in need of peeling,
what fish I choose for lunch
or how many times I dust the rooms?

No, no, awake or asleep
I dream, my love,
as most of us do.
Dream of golden horses in fields of cowslips,
peace in a land always beautiful
no wars, violence or hurt.

Like you, I withdraw from the world of reality
my hands grope for the path at night
my feet tread carefully to avoid lines.
Spaces fill with crotchets, quavers
a melody to rise
over dizzy mountain slopes
where prayer-wheels whirl and clatter
and rhododendrons riot.

Home Visit

For David Healey

It's the same for you, doctor,
she said,
all these pills and potions
spread out on the kitchen table
will do neither of us any good.

I am ready,
she said,
to turn my face to the wall

or to the east,
or to the sun .....
deeply sad, doctor,
that's the root of it.

And yet ....
the strawberries,
she said,
warm, slightly gritty,
fingers smelling sweet of them.
The grey dawns with bird chorus,
clip clop of horse
when coming home on a summer night,

my heart -
or was it yours, doctor?
turns over.

What you want
is the word made visible

or is that what I want?
Isn't that why you are here
to tell me?

Elizabeth Bewick

Heartsease

A warm night after rain, I step outside
and smell the new-washed air that emanates
from roses in the gardens of the town
and from the bedrooms where the young girls lie
wakeful in tented sheets, their hearts aflame
for lovers in their still undreamt-of dreams.
Another shower sends me back indoors
to my own garden mirrored in the rain;
I close the window in a sudden chill
and drink my cocoa in a spindrift shawl.

Morning again and pansies barely dry
are little battered flags of brilliance
growing in cracks between my paving stones.
Heartsease, you called them, and for love of you
I touch their petals with a gentle hand
and pick the weathered dead-heads carefully.

My garden is a meadow lush with weeds
in whose green depths such hidden flowers grow
as one day will suffice for all your needs.
I thought so once, sadly uncertain now
I cherish flowers that thrived on my neglect
and throw the weeds upon the rising heap.
Yet, in my seventieth year, I am ashamed
because of all the things I have not done,
the sins committed in my carelessness;
you told me once my greatest talent was
simply for loving, now I need to know
that heartsease pansies still have power to heal.

Patricia Bishop

Parabolas

Entering the church their face stretch,
their bodies poised sedate, distant.

I watch hands dipping
the shaking of water
that formal crossing.

They keep God in this barrel-vaulted space
filling altar and choir,
the gaps in the central-heating grilles,
the box 'of your charity'.

'Of your charity,
pray for the souls
of the dear-departed'

As a child I prayed for the forgotten.
Younger still, I thought the departed
left King's Cross for Edinburgh, flew North.

The people here kept to the rails
of their communion.
Shuffled between the stations of the cross
finding their own North.

I move my restless hands.
Long ago I tumbled out
into this freer, harsher place.

Now from its rocks
I watch their train grow smaller.

Tomorrow they'll be a fist of smoke.

Anne Born

Hooks

Iron hooks hung in rows
from the beams of the dark
end attic. No windows.
Walls of criss-crossed plaster.

If you went there
to fetch dusty china
or glasses sedimented
with dead spiders,

you went away fast.
Fingers of the air clammed
your face, a threat
breathed in your ear.

We left years ago.
The rows of hooks
are in my hair today.
I could feel my hams

had been hung there,
the stuck pig's scream
my fear. The locked-in child
sob-racked to silence.

Whatever hung there
suffers in perpetuity.
Hooked pigs, fish, people
never rest in peace.

A Dog's Life in Bosnia

Our home mortgaged to fear,
when I looked at the coffee-pot,
the dog's scratch on doors,
they weren't real, we'd lost
the right to ourselves.

Enemies held the key.
The children asked and asked
and I had no answers, tried
to play games
and lost every round.

I begged him to leave,
I knew he should. But nights,
together I was alone but still
alive. They came, of course,
took him outside . . .

We couldn't move for hours,
days. Then I made food,
held on to the children, afraid
to look in their eyes. I still am.
When friends came to help

I went outside to find him.
Then understood why the dog
had not been hungry. How
can I live? Why do you ask me
questions? I have no answers.

Pat Borthwick

The Scan

Together we explore my inner landscape on the screen.
He plots a course and charts me frame by frame.
See, here's your pancreas, your spleen, he chats,
And over here, this, the outline of your liver.

I watch my abdomen appear in monochrome.
Ghost-shapes float haloed, flickering like neon signs.
I expect Apollo to land, a space-suited man step out,
Glide strangely slowly across my contours with a flag.

The radiologist has moved his cursor, clicked.
The image on the monitor splits in two.
One half zooms in, zooms in again
To where circles bright as Saturn's rings

Cast hard-edged shadows stretching inbetween.
Mare Frigoris, Mare Nubrium, Sea of Cold,
Sea of Clouds, *Lacus Aestruum, Oceanus Procellarum,*
Seething Lake and Ocean of Storms.

I kneel behind a crater full of stars
As data ricochets across the voids. The spaceman
Plants his flag in the spot marked X, leaves moonboot tracks
Like 'cut-here' lines along my ovarian tract.

That night I'm in the orchard among the apple trees.
The hens have shaken out their duvets in the roots.
I slide my hand under a warmth of breast, find
A perfect egg to hold against the black. Obliterate the moon.

Jacqueline Brown

from: **Thinking Egg**

In the Room II

On blue paper sheeting
a woman is lying
on her side, knees to nose
like an ovenready chicken

another woman is stroking
her hand clenched till skin
feels close to tearing, like
she's a baby like she's a child

just relax if you can
clever girl   that's right

a man in a clean white coat's
an invisible voice moving
unseen in the greenpaint room
just a paper rustle, a mumble

she is not a clever girl
she is not a good girl
the snap of the rubber glove
condemns; the blue paper rucks
with her guilt

under a rubber membrane fingers
inquire, tamper - slick fingers
with no face eyes colour hair -
she has unbodied his fingers

Try to relax   it'll hurt less

a woman is severing a body into bits
guillotine snaps and the head floats
free, snap and snap through the pubic
bone and the body rises, next the legs;
on the blue paper sheet is a tiny pocket
of air encased in stoneskin and a wet
finger learning something and a mind
recording determined to forget

the other woman is helping her from the bed
saying *It's all right, it's all over,*
saying *There, dear* . . . but the silly eyes
can't not look at the map of Africa
damp-etched on the blue paper sheeting
can't not fast forward to all the miles
and miles to go . . . desert and sea
and desert and sea before the ghost
of a landing.

Poaching

*You could assemble a whole catalogue of 'do's and don'ts' on the subject
of poaching eggs . . . Don't attempt to poach more than two unless you're
a really experienced hand.*   Delia Smith's Cookery Course Part 1

She has heard the women whispering
in hospital rooms of suffering,
pain, blood.

She has stood palefaced in the margins
looking and listening, separate
from them.

While they slept, she has walked in her head
through the bluelit quiet ward, skirting
the nurse,

toe-stepped along the white corridor,
keeping to walls, to where milky kids
snuffle;

she's walked further to a flurried place
where infants lie flat under glass, taped
to tubes

Sleepwalking, she has understood theft,
the urge to prise open, steal and hide,
not care

that another woman is crying somewhere
just so long as her own boat of arms
is full.

Finality of Egg

whitecoated syllables in a hot quiet room
head listening, not hearing air become words
        sorry . . . a miracle . . . adoption . . . to terms
she hears somebody crying saying Oh no No

centuries later hearing her feet scrunch
through shingle not looking back   caught
eyes squint not to see the lozenge lights
off sunburnt sea no eyes air where mind was

home in a greenshade kitchen clockwork hands
shred chop slice whisk mix - can't not marvel
at hand design there in this caught minute
till aeons later the darkhaired man comes

flowers card a greenglass bottle of wine -
she had forgotten that other moment - two kids
in their twenties a plaster cake words loud
in a still silence her body weeps for what is lost

she has no body - a stone on a beach - she has
no eyes - seaglare has blinded she has no voice -
it can't be her voice saying *miracle adoption sorry*
while eggs surface bluely through white mayonnaise

Nadine Brummer

Hazel Nuts

Late August, pale and premature,
some lay in ruts below the hedge,
nestled in twin green bracts.
Rain or birds, the snap of twigs
had made them drop. Others ripened.
I found one sliced across the top
like a breakfast egg. I put it by -
a globe with a black hole inside.

Julian held in the palm of her hand
an item like a hazel nut,
and saw the whole world made and kept
forever. Only a mind in love
can see like that. I took leave
of my senses once, a nut-case
in a truckle bed. I keep it by -
this husk scooped clean.

Trouvaille or a trivial thing?
The more that I look into it
the more I see a hole
I can't see round. I'm perplexed;
my mind is more or less intact
but only a shell unless I find
a seed shaped like a globe inside
that nothing cracks.

Julian of Norwich, anchoress and mystic, 1342 - after 1416.

At the Lucian Freud Exhibition

Head, hands, genitals and feet
are main events - he does them well.
Excess between is fleshed, like meat.

And even now it takes some nerve to look
at turkey gizzards limp between men's legs
and women opening to a swarm of black.

Oh there's a buzz all right. Once at another show
I heard a woman in a hat enthuse
about a clever orchid, how

lips form a helipad for flies
which land in ruts, are trapped then sucked
where male and female parts are fused,

though none are needed for the helleborine
quite self-sufficient with its seed.
Can flowers be both gorgeous and obscene?

Leigh Bowery's back is overgrown with flecks,
an orchidaceous pink, buttocks sag
into an off-white stool. You sense the cracks

of old enamel bowls and chipped chrome taps
behind a drape. In front a red-brown rug
bristles. These genteel props

touch my eyes. Below each covering a frame,
upholding surfaces of this and that,
lies coiled, and I am forced to look again

at how I live. This cold October day
I'm in a crowd well-heeled and buttoned up
engrossed with such carnality

I fear our coats might flake and tear
and eyes, preoccupied with doubt,
find bodies we'd not bargained for.

Catherine Byron

Silk and Belfast Linen

I   The Lampshade Makers

First, a slow and ravelled bandaging
of wire, the soldered junctions awkward,
the frame a snare for their wrists,
and that flat card of cross-cut binding
a footling shuttle as they lay the tape's
raw edge round ferrous metal
that would else, in this sporey climate, oxidise.

And then they take their trousseaux
all to bits - all their night things
snip-snipped to a panel pattern:
the camisoles and wedding negligées
of silk and silk-satin and silk mousseline.
They cut away chafed seams, stained underarms,
faint foxing of blood below.

Oh, there are stretches that are good
as new, blush pink and peachy!
These they seam into a sleeve of silk
and raise a taut pavilion.
                              Now
silk's in eclipse until its lamp is lit.

II   Shears

In the linen mills I was a weaver of linen.
(That was before I married Billy Morrow.)
My own loom, uh huh, my own web.
Them was great times. Forty of us girls
pedalling Belfast linen on forty looms.

But yer man - Robinson, was it? - would saunter along
the aisle of the looms. Didn't he have the quick eye
for a slub in the damask, even a thickened thread.
He had soft hands. The other checkers'd point
so as you could mend it. Robinson? Oh no.

His wee white nail'd
pick and pick and pick
till that slub was a hole in the web
and the pink prick of his finger
poked right through.

'Yon's a fault!' Robinson dandered his shears
handy like, at his belt. In four snips
he'd cut the warp in two. 'That'll larn ye.'

Mebbe a day's piece gone. Mebbe a week's.
Whatever it was, it was a ruin of linen.
Priceless. The girl wageless. And in debt for the yarn.

III   Pegging Out

I was snapping the creases from damp linen
and damp cotton, making small bangs
of the sort the wind makes when it's hard
on the clothes, and they give off reports like a flag
or even a whip.
                        As I stretched one pillowcase
crack! It ripped in ten places
all parallel in a laddery sort of run:
the last of our wedding linen.

The frame of drawn threadwork's still intact,
that for twenty-five years was a dotted line
for no one to tear along.

It's the body that's given way, the holder of pillow,
worn by the rub of ears, abrasion of hair, by pillowtalk
and washing, washing, washing.

                              I thought
of my mother and father, still pulling and snapping
sheets between them after forty-nine years
and I laughed, laugh now at my freedom
out there in the silvery weather of the falling year.

Fat Hen

You ask me to plough the ground: shall I
take a knife and tear my mother's bosom?
You ask me to cut grass and make hay and
sell it and be rich like white men; but how
dare I cut my mother's hair?
                    Smohalla, a 19th century Native American

Today, when I went out to garden, the bare soil
of my small clearing distressed me. That earth is distressed.
I have scraped it, and shaken it by the shoulders: 'What!
letting in goosegrass again?' I've warned it - how
many times? - not to cradle weeds. It doesn't learn.

                    Our daughter, even at ten
would follow me in the furrows to pick up the wounded,
her field hospital a row of plastic pots
where they lingered, astonished exotics:

Chickweed.   Dandelion.   Horsetail.

For years since I've persisted in wringing their necks
in the abattoir of my weeding, taken a blade
that is not the blade of harvest, and run them through.
Weeds fall with no sound or struggle. Not
like the old layer whose head came off in your hand.
She staggered about the yard over and over
dragging her whites in the jugular spangles of red.

Today, I walked back to the house that you have left
between grasses I have long since ceased to mow
and I wished I could sweep like a Buddhist the path before me
lest my feet in falling should crush
                    any creature,
any creature.

Sally Carr

Soft Fruit

Green and hard as marbles
they roll into the bowl. The hairs
like the bristles we joked
about on her spinster chin.

As I lift the skirts of bushes,
the fruit tucked out of sight,
I remember Nellie. Did she consider
secretly, fruit's moist creases,
soft sacs, spurting juice? The blonde
halo of bloom on her sweetheart's
scarcely shaveable face?

On the mantel-piece she kept
a khaki photograph of a young
soldier from the Great War.
She never mentioned his name.

Each year I fill the same vessels
with ruched, bruisable scarlet
and lustrous bubbles of blood,
the hard-to-shift dye on my fingers
like the mess of life's miracles:
first shock at thirteen, then birth
and the whisked away placenta,
years later above my daughter
the purple fruit of transfusion
and on the floor by her bed a jar
slowly filling with strained red,
a liquor full-bodied as claret.

I bend next to pick currants -
strings of dark beads in a basin -
and imagine the young man
in the field hospital: his wounds,
the crimson splashes on the white
enamel of the kidney bowl,
the soaked dressings the colour
of Nellie's summer pudding.

Liz Cashdan

Wool Trade

Wool was my staple.
For two generations, my grandfather's firm
Elias Trilling and Son, traded raw wool.
Evading pogrom in Bialystok, revolution in Moscow
they travelled and bargained
till Samuel, the son, came to England,
sorting oily bales in dark-roomed offices,
fingering grey wool in dark blue wrappers.
Always tidy in his white clinical coat,
assessing quality, risking orders,
sending telegrams about weights and prices,
he failed with the slump, but regained his losses.

In my silver spoon-fed childhood
words from the wool trade, noil and shoddy,
teased and carded from greasy wool
wove a protecting blanket, warm, patterned,
like the brown rugs from the Bialystok factory.
While on Hampstead's shivering cobbles
rickety kids played backstreet, shoeless
and took our old clothes.

Alison Chisholm

Swimming with Dolphins

Gunmetal gleam of wet flank
swirls, leaps, corkscrews
water charged. I paddle shallows,
not daring the slipstream.

A bolder voice cries 'Dive!'
I stay skin deep, swim dipping,
finding reassurance in the scrunch
of shells beneath my feet.
Wrack wraps itself around my legs,
oozes at thighs, reaches.

At once I see
that I have glutted on familiar things,
walked grass and gravel, smelled wet earth,
known taste of peach and honey.

I am drawn
to different consummation,
learning shifting silt and brine,
salt smack and fish:
and at the epicentre of new chaos
dolphins thrust their pewter,
grinning welcome.

First strokes are hesitant, but soon
I cleave wave swell, surrender
self to water, surge each crest
with spray in starburst droplets
shaken from my hair, my skin.

At one with dolphins,
I am ready now
to stride taut flesh, ride eddies,
plunge where undreamed currents call.

Gillian Clarke

Miracle on St David's Day

'They flash upon that inward eye
Which is the bliss of solitude'
- The Daffodils by W. Wordsworth

An afternoon yellow and open-mouthed
with daffodils. The sun treads the path
among cedars and enormous oaks.
It might be a country house, guests strolling,
the rumps of gardeners between nursery shrubs.

I am reading poetry to the insane.
An old woman, interrupting, offers
as many buckets of coal as I need.
A beautiful chestnut-haired boy listens
entirely absorbed. A schizophrenic

on a good day, they tell me later.
In a cage of first March sun a woman
sits not listening, not seeing, not feeling.
In her neat clothes the woman is absent.
A big, mild man is tenderly led

to his chair. He has never spoken.
His labourer's hands on his knees, he rocks
gently to the rhythms of the poems.
I read to their presences, absences,
to the big dumb, labouring man as he rocks.

He is suddenly standing, silently,
huge and mild, but I feel afraid. Like slow
movement of spring water or the first bird
of the year in the breaking darkness,
the labourer's voice recites 'The Daffodils'.

The nurses are frozen, alert; the patients
seem to listen. He is hoarse but word-perfect.
Outside the daffodils are still as wax,
a thousand, ten thousand, their syllables
unspoken, their creams and yellows still.

Forty years ago, in a Valleys school,
the class recited poetry by rote.
Since the dumbness of misery fell
he has remembered there was a music
of speech and that once he had something to say.

When he's done, before the applause, we observe
the flowers' silence. A thrush sings
and the daffodils are flame.

Ark

'Keeping the seed alive upon the face of all the earth once the
fountains of the deep and the windows of the sky are stopped.'
Genesis

1

Winter of rain, the rivers of Europe too big for themselves,
and the oceans rising. The sea's at the door. It curls into the cellar,
climbs the stairs, laps the threshold of cities.
Coastal towns go under. A church falls to the waves.
Only the watchman awake to cry 'flood' in the drunken palace
as the wall is breached and the sea takes Cantre'r Gwaelod.
Only a boy with his thumb in the dyke as the low countries drown.

2

From Oxfam, an ark of gopher wood,
each beast so crude I can't name it for sure:
elephant, tiger, zebra, two maned lions, no lioness,
white creatures tall as camels or giraffes.
Could they be sheep?

3

Rain falls through February, March.
'Of every clean beast thou shall take to thee by sevens.'
Beulah Speckle-faced, and three black faced ewes.
The flock puddles the field to mud.
We wake nightly in the early hours, dress for the rain,
to count their faces in the flashlight, their glittering eyes.

A sudden day of light and the March wind's home
like a hare running. The flock is moonlit cloud,
their breath starlight. One ewe stands alone
turning and turning, pawing the ground.
The horizons in the gold-green of her eyes
know the midwife in me before I do.

You hold her shoulders and talk tenderly.
The scalding cave's familiar as soapy washing,
in my hand a sodden head, the slippery pebbles
of hooves. Out of the bone ark adrift
on its flood I bring the lamb. Its skull
is the moon on my palm,

the four of us murmuring, earthed again,
getting our bearings.

The Field-Mouse

Summer, and the long grass is a snare drum.
The air hums with jets.
Down at the end of the meadow,
far from the radio's terrible news,
we cut the hay. All afternoon
its wave breaks before the tractor blade.
Over the hedge our neighbour travels his field
in a cloud of lime, drifting our land
with a chance gift of sweetness.

The child comes running through the killed flowers,
his hands a nest of quivering mouse,
its black eyes two sparks burning.
We know it'll die, and ought to finish it off.
It curls in agony big as itself
and the star goes out in its eye.
Summer in Europe, the fields hurt,
and the children kneel in long grass
staring at what we have crushed.

Before day's done the field lies bleeding,
the dusk garden inhabited by the saved, voles,
frogs, a nest of mice. The wrong that woke
from a rumour of pain won't heal,
and we can't face the newspapers.
All night I dream the children dance in grass,
their bones brittle as mouse-ribs, the air
stammering with gunfire, my neighbour turned
stranger, wounding my land with stones.

from: **Glass**

At the Glass Factory

The recipe is lead, sand, fire,
dangerous treacles spun for the tourists.
Before our eyes a goblet forms
in the sun-shaft of particles burning
with light off the Lagoon.
It stills to ice, becomes
contained stillness,
a canal of smoky water,
cupful of light ready
to be burnished with a clean white cloth.

Her Table

She fussed between kitchen and dining room
giving us all things to carry and do.
I see her two hands polishing a wine glass
until it gleams, immaculate.
She lifts it to the light and sets it down
on starched damask on the Christmas table.

On an ordinary Sunday it would be
a cut-glass jug of water, four tumblers.
As if these things could hold us, as if
they could make us flawless and ring true.

Anne Cluysenaar

from: **Vaughan Variations**

10

'What emanations
Quick vibrations
And bright stars are there?'
'Midnight'

Midday.

The sheep lie
on the high ground.

This is their habit,
to seek a vantage
before they sleep.

The hills from this height,
and the valley, look shadowless,
as if light from within
had replaced the sun.

Surfaces familiar,
lovely, of home,
lose definition.
The skin no longer
limits or touches.

It seems. It seems
a rolling meniscus,
holding only just.
Pressed between different
densities. Fragile
immense location.

Of which awareness
comes as it is broken.
Weight returns.
The thin circle
of grass-blade and shadow
on a stone by my head
trembles a little.

Nothing to be afraid of.
I can smell the warm
ewe's wool as a lamb
butts and suckles.
For me too
a place waits
in which love can be
natural as death.

And better it is
for that other, though what
that other may be
formula and word
both fail. It is
like a breath, like
eating and drinking are
(extensions of matter).
Like making love.

How could Henry believe
that an orphan lad
shepherding on the mountain
saw a youth garlanded
in green? Who loosed
a hawk (as he slept)
which flew through his mouth
to his inward parts,
so he woke gifted
with fear and poetry.

16

On the sudden death of a friend's wife.

'But life is, what none can express.'
        Quickness

After the first shock, days
of (despite myself) thinking
'it could not have happened'
then raising my eyes and
being astonished instead that
the world was still there
and myself still seeing it.

In one of those first days
we saw her, the white doe,
slowly stepping between
the pine-dark edge
and a bright bulge of pasture
along our furthest fence.
One, two, three steps
only, as she passed,
moving only her long legs
behind the tiers of may-blossom.

By the time I got over there
to see if I could catch
sight of her still standing,
maybe, among the tree-trunks -
dark uprights of them floating
among bluebells, thickening
one behind the other until
no more spaces could be imagined -
there wasn't a sign of her:
no tuft on the barbed wire
and the grass wasn't silver
where her hooves might have brushed it.

Was this the place? Or further
along the fence - perspectives
being what they are and we
too excited to count fence-posts?
And then against the light,
there were soft holes
in the grass, no more than that.
Her step had been so high,
so certain, as she passed.

I stood between the near scent
of the may and the vast wafting
dimness of so many bluebells.
My husband gone back in the house,
there was nothing to see but
the edge of an empty field and
a woman standing at the edge.

I found it hard to imagine
the weight of the doe, so flat
and white she looked, stepping
in profile behind the may,
her neck vertical as a periscope.
Any warmth she had breathed
into this air, invisible now,
must be drifting with the pale seeds
of the sallow in a great bank
of slow-moving forest breath.

In spite of myself, I strained
after a hint of hesitating white.
There was just a blueness there,
a rise and fall of distance
among closing trees. Dim
but, when focused on, intense.

Stilled

At the Natural History Museum
For George Beccaloni

Pinned on the tray,
    his wings outspread,
        still and dry:
            Ornithoptera croesus croesus.

'This may be the actual one'
    you tell me, angling the glass -
        the sooty texture
            of immense wings
                dazzles by its darkness.

Somewhere on the body
    forensic signs, maybe,
        of Wallace's careful fingers
as he drew this butterfly, living,
    from the net? And his own heart
        sent blood rushing,
            so that 'I felt
much more like fainting
    than I have done
        when in apprehension
            of immediate death' -
all day afterwards,
    ah, how his head ached!

To that *Mussaenda* shrub
    with its white bracts and long
        yellow orange-eyed blooms,
            lured by scent and sight,
                croesus would come for nec

Closed up, he'd make just a patch
    of leaf-thrown shadow,
        or an oblong black-veined leaf,
            yellow-green in sunlight.

Open, the bright petals
    on his outspread wings -
        orange sprays, yellow dots,
            amid yellow and white and orange -
would hold his body safe
    in a bill-distracting corolla.

As I catch a trace
    of Wallace's fine-tipped quill
        on the tiny round of the label
and the dull glint of the pin
    through that wizened thorax,
I think of a mind's movement
    stilled between pages,
        as dead, as rich -

ready in another mind
    to fly, and settle.

Alfred Russel Wallace (1823-1913), co-discoverer with Darwin of the
theory of natural selection, explored the Malay Archipelago, finding
new or rare species including the magnificent birdwing butterfly
Ornithoptera croesus croesus. This poem is from a sequence dedicated
to the memory of Wallace. The quotations are from his autobiography.

Gladys Mary Coles

The Glass Island

(Ynys-Witrin or Glastonbury)

1. The Legends

A green lagoon; marshes, reed-mazed,
and a long boat gliding like the swans,
the quiet swans drawing their invisible chariot
towards the otherworld, the glass island.

And the long boat arriving nudges the grassy banks
where the only sound is the whispered sound
of voyagers from a time before, their circular call
to those, water-crossing, who come ashore.

Centuries of comings, season by season -
the grail-seekers, the pilgrims
leaving no trace on light and air.

The white perpetuation of belief:
a midwinter thorn blossoming
each ice-time in the melt-meadows;
a windfall of bones in a buried oak
'here lie Arthur and golden Guinevere'.

Words and wood and water -
water a reservoir of beginnings
speaking of pre-beginnings.

2. The Well

A liquid torc around the neck
of a pilgrim, reflected, drinking
from the chalice of earth.

3. The Tor

Rising above other domes of grass,
above Wearyall and Windmill,
the island of glass under an unreal geography
of clouds, shape-shifting, pulled apart.
Cloud-drift, constantly dispersing,
reassembling, like the seekers who come
season by turning season: they wind
a spiral way up vestigial paths
and fade one by one
imperceptibly as the wild geese
flying high at twilight.

Heat, marsh-light and the glass island
glistening behind the sun's incense.
What shines is neither grail nor chalice
but sharp-edged shards, a glazed bead,
a fragment of window, water in a glass.

Late August Fireworks, Llandudno Bay

The tide hangs fire, on a ten o'clock turn;
crowds, in the blustery dark, anticipate
pink flares, cascading sputniks, a false dawn.

We huddle under awnings, watch night-cloud
as the first shower of stars explodes, fades out:
successive wonders rise and are devoured.

Above the Great Orme's flood-lit cliffs and woods
detonations splatter the Celtic west,
denote real firepower in troubled worlds.

Our minds meander when the magic palls:
though lasers colour the sky, write in light,
I see childhood's embers, collapsing fires.

My father sees war-searchlights cross, re-cross,
two bombers hit, in flames, their crews bale out -
falling through air four effigies which blaze.

My mother thinks of far galactic stars
named after gods; November gardens split
by bonfires; damp squibs and burnt-out cases.

The final burnished rain fans out, then dies:
we're faced with smoky darkness; all that's left
the jewelled pier, the black incoming waves.

After Edgehill, 1642

(for Peter Holmes)

1. Villagers Report *The Late Apparitions*

A December Saturday, star-clear,
at Kineton. Three months since the battle,
the village collects itself - Christmas
perhaps a demarcation, a control
in the blood-letting. Yet on the ridge
of Edge Hill, the night resounds,
armies grinding one against the other
re-enacting the action, re-dying the deaths.

Shepherds hear trumpets, drums -
expect a visitation of holy kings with retinues.
Instead, the spectral soldiers strike,
icy night skies crack with cries,
steel clashing and the sput of muskets.
A knot of Kineton men watch, witness;
Samuel Marshall, the Minister, says
the Devil's apparitions seize the dead.

2. A Ghost Speaks

I am unplanted, my world this waste -
the heath where bone was split, undressed of flesh,
where arteries unleashed their flood, the colour
of death. What is the colour of honour? The blue
in which we dissolve into air? the white of ashes?
Can I be woven into the braids of her hair, my lady,
or exist in the quick of my son's fingernails?
I, who carried the Standard, once drove the plough,
turning up earth, the harvest of worms. Now I envy
the seeds in the furrow, their dark cradle.

My blood is this Midlands field, this hacked hedgerow
where I lie, hearing the drumbeat of the dead,
corpses strewn rotting, graveless.
I glide up and down these rows of human manure,
the faces of soldiers like fallen cameos.
Here is Sir Edmund Verney, Thomas Transome -
they look skywards, lolling near my own wistful face.
Sir Edmund is grimacing slightly as he did in life,
Thomas Transome's skull a broken eggshell.

The brittle linnet flies from me. Dry leaves relinquish
their hold on twigs. A hare sits motionless, watching,
listening to last groans forever in the wind.
I see a troop of Horse on the skyline - Parliament's.
They charge our pikemen; now they vanish
like moving cloud-shadows across the field.
I cannot follow the clouds; I am chained to my carcass
hovering, as others are, above their unburied selves.

3. A Dragoon Observes Colonel Cromwell

Like a falcon from the gauntlet, he throws off these deaths.
He tells us 'Smile out to God in Praise', for his is the sword
of the Lord. I see his horse, piebald with blood.

Leafburners

move quietly as smoke
to their mounds; brush
rhythmically, apply spikes
to the invoices of winter,
papery tokens of decay

others wield spades like spoons
with the ease of breakfasters
shovelling cornflakes

when the pyre is high
they strike matches avidly:
in the wind of flames
dry leaves curl, given movement
for the last time

usually at dusk, gathering
in the corners of gardens,
servants to impalpable fire
they feed the autumn bier

eyes blazing with immolation,
their office skills, creeds, degrees
fall away, severed boughs
tossed to crackle, burn
and, in burning, change

the earth the air receives

Wendy Cope

By the Round Pond

You watch yourself. You watch the watcher too -
A ghostly figure on the garden wall.
And one of you is her, and one is you,
If either one of you exists at all.

How strange to be the one behind a face,
To have a name and know that it is yours,
To be in this particular green place,
To see a snail advance, to see it pause.

You sit quite still and wonder when you'll go.
It could be now. Or now. Or now. You stay.
Who's making up the plot? You'll never know.
Minute after minute swims away.

Les Vacances

(Walter Richard Sickert, *Bathers, Dieppe,* 1902,
Walker Art Gallery, Liverpool)

Maman et Papa au bord de la mer.
Aujourd'hui il fait beau. I remember it well.
Voilà Armand, in the corner down there,
With Maman et Papa au bord de la mer!
Oh, bored, c'est le mot. I tear out the hair
As we limp through ce livre avec Mademoiselle.
Maman et Papa au bord de la mer.
Il fait beau. I remember it only too well.

The Lavatory Attendant

Slumped on a chair, his body is an S
That wants to be a minus sign.

His face is overripe Wensleydale
Going blue at the edges.

In overalls of sacerdotal white
He guards a row of fonts

With lids like eye patches. Snapped shut
They are castanets. All day he hears

Short lived Niagaras, the clank
And gurgle of canescent cisterns.

When evening comes he sluices in a thin tide
Across sand coloured lino,

Turns Medusa on her head
And wipes the floor with her.

Elsa Corbluth

Dirge for St. Patrick's Night

Rain on the red roses:
I had a daughter. I have none.
Grey fog on green hills rises:
I had two children. I have one.

Mist on the scented blossom:
she left, one afternoon,
face a flower, body lissom:
the same night burnt to bone.

Needing to tend the needy,
so as to find, and touch, Christ,
she reached his home unready
for this mocking of her trust.

Flowers of flame flourished redly
in her window while she slept:
love of dead Christ proved deadly,
her youth and my joy trapped.

Jesus said, suffer children,
not black-stick skeletons.
God's Joan or devil's cauldron?
Ash, all the holy ones.

At her grave's head, pale roses
picked with their claws of blood:
eighteen summers' slain praises,
under wet grass lies her God.

I use no words: no-one listens.
I use no tears with no ending.
My one girl the rain christens,
gutted house beyond mending.

Tricia Corob

from: India Notebook

Afternoons

For a moment they ride on light
their bicycle wheelspokes a white blaze
as they cross the sun's pathway

whereas those on foot - the bandy-legged beggar
two carpet traders from Colva
then the tangerine vendor, her basket on her head -

blacken like overripe fruit, melt to silhouettes
then reconfigure on the sand
a moment later. It's a sequence of fade-outs

and re-appearances and makes me wonder about us -
how soon we'll be burned out
and disassembled. And will we re-emerge

another lifetime perhaps, on the same sand - the fishing boats
asleep in the heat, the green of a sari flowing
and find it all oddly familiar? Back

under the café awning: *you want cold drink?*
The buffalo in the parched field
the crows keep redefining silence.

Hilary Davies

from: **When the Animals Came**

Autumn

When do the animals come?

After the great heat and the midge time
On the rivers are done. In the season
When the air's no longer dense with the thrum of insects
Or tern cry, the metamorphosis comes.
Each one of us locates it differently - a speckling on the leaves
Whirled from the birches, the ripening of the dark rowanberries,
The grilse quickening to come up river
The steppe bursting open like a fruit underfoot.

          We know then come the mists,
Weeklong exhaled like fire from the summer river,
A burning, consuming assumption of water into the air,
And the forest is hung with green glass.
This is the still time, the time when between heat and moisture
The trees seem to strain to a voice we don't hear,
The leaves all taut as if strung on a bow.
We lie exhausted in the nervous woodland,
Waiting the first mark of change,
The slow uncurling of an aspen leaf that bellows
In seconds to stormwind, baying and snapping
The tree crowns before it as reindeer go down before wolves.
We know fear then, nor cower never so close to the earth
But the sky spits phosphorescence, and the horizons
Boom like a thousand precipices exploding from the cliffs.
The night rains sweep in cold air;
The forest settles.

          It's then that the animals come.

*****

How do the animals come?

                              I'll tell you how I saw it as a youth -
My first hunt, so stationed with my father
Along the river bed, and told to watch.
The reconnaissance parties of the younger men
Sleep on the plain, hard to the elements,
Turning their faces, all day, all night long
Eastwards, licking the wind for the first signs of ice.
In the dark, you can hear them chanting, laughing
To chase the apprehension from their hearts;
Below, the tribe refines and overhauls equipment:
Burins, scalpels, missile projectors; the clack, clack,
Clack of stone on stone and sound of many voices
Rising from the autumnal foliage up to the watchmen on the rocks.
Make the channel here, the funnel guiding down
The gully to the fording place, cut back the branches,
Let the treacherous light through
To where the enticing water glitters and leads down.
Make sure this way they come.

Still full of sleep and early morning,
The kinsmen cooking, mothers picking lice,
When the frightened mouths yell down the rockface
'Now!' I take my station by the river trees
And watch the men come out. All hard hunters,
The tight-sinewed and the massive-muscular,
Those who cunningly tell the places, even though pot-bellied,
The hungriest, most recently admitted, with their javelin arm
Too hastily flung back. Greased and dressed towards their labours
They picket stealthily along the stream and prime their weapons.
The dew falls in their hair.
Birds chirrup, then sit, still; we hear a rustling
Where the women corral their children towards the shelters
And turn their chattering in upon the rock.
The strangest of all silences fell then; though nothing
In the crack and spit of things, the leaves' whisper
Or faint catching of the tide upon the gravelbanks
Was altered, it was as if the very tension
Of those minds placed there raised up a presence

From the valley floor who, gigantesque, passed from us
Between the fir trees and, with one gesture of his massive hand,
Threw down the die of fate.

Now the air cracks: the far boom of hooves
Unrolling forwards is like the striding of a tidal wave
Out from where continents shock.
Thus the army of desire for south, for west,
For warmth, approaches, and we step to meet it.

Interminably long. The river starts to sizzle.
At last the leader treads with caution over the cliff scree
And down; we hear the scratch of fetlocks as the deer dig in
To slow the drop. Their heat's upon us;
We can feel their breath. The young keep close
Beneath their mothers' bellies; the bulls ride, wary, pendulous,
Along the edges of the trail. And still the mother of the herd,
Who knows the landscape and the destination,
Glides them down the mudpath to the healing water.
Among the trees hands sweat upon the javelins,
And still the wily female guides, and fails,
And leads them to their death.

We go for the young, much much easier to kill.
How they scream! How much they want to live!
Their tongues twist purple round their muzzles,
Their mothers roar a roar you never heard.
Thus we turn them under the water with harpoon,
Assegai, hourlong; the soft river
Slips away with their soft blood.

*****

The hunt is finished. Till a late figure
Descends, snorting, through the aspen wood -
An old bull, setting us a prize - we jostle
For position as he hesitates, perturbed and anxious,
Flaring danger at the water's edge;
The warriors also, each stepping now the camp fire dance
Of animal and sorcerer for real.

But desire must outstalk fear: the bull must go
South with his females to the grazing lands;
The young, the glory-hungry hunters show themselves.
He crashes forward in an arc of sunlit water,
Emerging from a maze of falling gold
To bid for life. Across the flat, smooth rocks
One man snaps out, his eyes upon the furling dewlap -

The prize! the prize! - wrongfoots his dance,
And falls among the tides. Beneath the hooves,
The massive withers, he's rolled and pounded round the current,
His jaw and breastbone sifted to the sea.

Angela Dove

Carolina Crachami's Skeleton

Carolina Crachami was exhibited during her lifetime as 'The Sicilian Fairy' and is thought to have been about five years old when she died. Her 21 inch high skeleton was anatomised and is still displayed in the Hunterian Museum.

First he undressed
your tiny body, like a miniature bride.
Loosened the corset
and bustle of grubby white silk,
greasy fingermarks across belly
and breast. Lifted like a trophy,
passed from hand to hand,
dwarf child, I can hear the jokes

when he opened you.
And now I view his work, for where are
you in these bones? Tethered like an
extinct bird, no face to search for pain,
or love. Only a label with your name and height.
I stoop to read the fastidious hand.
I, who at your age

wandered museums alone,
opening doors, hungry for grown up
conversation. And found a still-room,
an unfamiliar smell of formalin,
and a man crouched
over a stone sink, hands plunged
into a soup of feathers, wishbone,
membrane, trying to get a hold,
hauling out something slippery;
complicated, yet as delicate
as the inner casing of a lychee skin.

And then he turned,
surprised by my question, replying
like a parent struggling to explain a dirty word
they wished they hadn't said,
*see it's a swan! the skin turned inside out,
here's the beak and here's the legs.*

Jane Duran

Forty Eight

Once a month I expect that I am pregnant.
My body takes that liberty -
in the street I am full of misgivings, armfuls,
my breasts manage the joy of being painful.

I expect that the gleaning has taken hold,
the warrior gates have closed
and the town turned heavy inside
with its gold, its tarnish of silver.
I expect the little known
to be drumming and corded,
my belly to be amazed and striated
with new boundaries.

There will be no going back,
once a month.
Nowhere will the bereft be local.
They will not be in their usual cafés.
They will be overlooking seaports
and their voices will drop with evening
so as not to wake the children.
No one will be childless
nor the haze hide a bay.

There are slip landings in my belly,
the tug of the mollusc love,
its impersonal kiss unfolded
its wish-kiss lying low
left behind when the sea goes out and stops
for my foot to go oops on the slippery rock.

When the blood lies out on its shoal,
when the blood arrives
on the sloop, on the stoop, like a sailor,
like an acrobat, like electricity,
I will say it is not really that.
No, no. I am not ready.

The Orange Tree in Cordoba

The gradual branches
just made out, grains, smudges,
the orange tree, its energy
behind a wall where children
gather, its sticky, searing juices,
its dust coming from nowhere
like a moment of sadness,
its branches laid softly
against women, like menstruation.

A girl comes down the steps.
There are summers still in her,
there is oil and bead on her.
She holds her child's hand.
Lavenders wash the streets
with their browns in the early
mornings in Cordoba.

To the cry of the childless
the orange tree answers with fruit,
to the suppressed cry of the childless
the mementoes of its armfuls,
to the red and white striped arches
of the womb, the sky hurrying past
the lilies of the womb, it answers
'There is nothing more to be done.

The long robes of air
drag the earth like bloodstains
like the caked hoofs of horses,
the blacksmiths harrying the horseshoes
the Moors leaving Cordoba endlessly.

Nine-month, nine-month lanterns
never so extinct as now.
Go into the Mosque.
Feel the power of space inside you,
the insatiable leaf-turning hand.'

Maestrazgo

The deeper I go in the wind
the more unreal the days of departure
till I reach a look-out point
over distant farmhouses, sheepfolds

and see the waterline of the mountain range
as if it were part of me,
the friendliness and force it exerts on me.

My father said goodbye. He joined the militia.
Everything is lifted up and dries.
It is a long way down
from all parched things.

Battle of Teruel, Winter 1937-38

I could write books about my father's books.
There was no dust on them. He held them in his hands
as if for the last time. They were quilted,
poised for their moment, shoved in one by one
till they made a smooth wall - one book, all one.

They stole out in golds, in secret reds
as if with a cigarette in the early morning
before the mist has cleared absolutely
into pitilessness. You could touch the titles
and they would be important.

In the dark of them - personal boundaries,
edges he had stepped so close to,
the icy hill over the valley, soldiers clinging
to the slopes, seams of snow,
the Spain he held and held to,
line after line giving way.

Jean Earle

Two Rhondda Valley Poems

1. 1926 Strike

How sad, the rag-and-bone man's horn
Lifted on high....
Tooted with a wry neck,
Sidewise from his flat cart.

The sound hung on afternoons
Of few blackberries,
In littered dingles where we played.
Men picking coal on tips
Caught the tinny blare
Coming and going. Gone.

Blow to the heart,
A known mock. Women listened
At closed doors.

Rags... and bones.

2. Living With It

After certain weather,
The bracken purpled
Dark and beautiful, to the moraine colour
Of people's hearts

That broke, slowly,
Hidden in bone and decently.

Managing mostly without weddings
But at funerals showing
Close purple,
Slashed with iron's red.

The Fox

Lightfoot on loneliness,
A winter fox

Not hunted
But as the true light in fur is,
Each hair a spirit
Of the whole radiance.
Light and the woods
And revelation
Come all together, as though prophesied.

Later, in weariness,
I dreamed a fox
Running on sparkle. Delicate tread
Indented trackings of mastodon,
Dinosaur - back and back
To infinity's edge. And there, the fox sprang off
Into the dark. I saw his diamond brush
Illuminate nothingness.
These imprints faded,
Fused into man's with links of holy fire.

This was the long-expected comet,
Emanuel, God-with-us.

I had not thought
To see that in my time - and was asleep
Only a minute.

Stillborn

There was a child born dead.

Time has bleached out the shocking insult.
Ageing has cicatrised the body's wound.

Still I do not like to prune bushes
That push to the sun...
Nor put my brush into the spider's house
Where she keeps her children,
Darting with terrible life.

With reluctance, I gouge potatoes
Sprouting intently in a dark bag.

Furtive, I slip one into the earth,
'Grow!' I say. 'Grow, if you must...'

Christine Evans

Bluebells in Nanhoron

Their rising unlatches the season.
Bright as flesh, as easy bruised, they gather
Even in snow, shards of a mirror

Where other selves drunk on their honeys
Harvest and grieve over armfuls
Or, dubbed with sap in their deep cool bed

Dizzy-ringed with love and deepest-vein blue,
Hug a slow way home as the hardfaced moon
Melts and lies down in the whispering aisles.

Like ours, their roots are naked. Bare as tubes
Not gripping or resisting, they suck
Last year's sugar, feed this summer back.

Slowly the canopy closes.
In its caves, birdsong first echoes
Then falls hushed. Curt with seed

The dry stalks rattle, ended. Yet this afternoon
A letter tells me *Driving Mother back*
To the Home in Wolverhampton

By Nant we stopped and wound the windows down
So she might smell the bluebells.
We could not tell if it was now she'd seen

Or a wood long bulldozed under, but slow tears
Rinsed her eyes and she cried out
Of blue, like mist, and special sharp-edged green.

For an hour she talked with sense and without pain
Of lives and places eighty years behind.
We never thought so much could have remained.

Ruth Fainlight

The Lace-wing

Does the lace-wing see me? I stare
Into its pinpoint ruby eyes, head on,
At its bristly mouthparts, my nose brushing antennae.

When I look away the lace-wing turns
Abruptly, as if dismissed or freed.
Its shoulder-pivot swings a thread-leg forward.
It moves briskly across my paper,
Then disappears under a corner.

The intensity of our mutual
Examination exhausted me.
We almost exchanged identities.
Our pupils throbbed with the same shared
Awe, acknowledgement, and curiosity.
We met beyond confine of size or species.

Next day, the lace-wing still is here.
It clings to the window-frame, drinking
Sunlight. It survives for its moment.
And what sustains our two existences
Remains as much a mystery as God.

Aeneas' Meeting with the Sibyl

Hunched over rustling leaves spread out
before her on the stony ground, like a skinny
gypsy with a joint dripping ash in the corner of her mouth
quizzing the Tarot cards, pulling the shabby
shawl closer round elbows and shoulders, then squinting
shrewdly sideways up at a nervous client,
the Sibyl greeted Aeneas. 'Don't tell it from them,'
he pleaded. She was sitting cross-legged, right at the door
of her cave, and he'd heard how often the wind (Apollo!
he thought, it's draughty here, no wonder she looks
so pinched and cold) shuffled the leaves into total

confusion, which she didn't seem to notice or
amend. 'Don't show them to me. Say it in words.'

'You're all the same,' she grumbled. 'Always wanting
more than you pay for. Of course'- tilting her head
sideways on that mole-strewn stringy neck
(he saw white hairs among the dusty curls)
an inappropriate cajoling smile
distorting her archaic features - 'if you give me
something extra,' she wheedled, 'I'll do you a special.'
The tattered russet-purple layers of skin
and cloth wrapped around her body dispersed
an ancient odour of sweat or incense as her movements
stirred them. Through a hole in the skirt he glimpsed a lean
and sinewy thigh, and feet bound up in rags.
'Come inside, young man,' she ordered. 'We'll be private there.'

Remembering what came next: his search for the golden
bough, their descent into Hades, the twittering shades,
his painful meeting with Dido, the Sibyl's answer
to Palinurus, and then, at last, embracing
Anchises his father, and learning the destiny
of their descendants, the future of Rome,
Aeneas found it hard to reconcile
his first impressions with the awesome figure
who led him safely through the realm of death
and to the daylight world again. He looked
back from the shore to where she crouched outside
her cave, waiting for another questioner,
and saw she had assumed the same disguise.

U.A. Fanthorpe

Kinch & Lack
(Boys' Outfitters)

Elderly man with a tape-measure.
Pedantic; a shade arch
(I don't see this at the time),
Treats my brother like a bride.

My mother not at ease
(I feel, but don't know why);
My brother, flattered, diffident,
Somehow aware of destiny.

Youngest son faces his kingdom
And his trousseau, socks, cap, scarf,
Wreathed in official colours
For unimagined deeds,

Greek, rugger, chemistry, things
He will do and I shan't,
Though I am two years older,
Taller, have read more books.

He's rehearsed for a special future
By a man with pins in his mouth;
Seven-year Dante, whose Vergil
Salutes his inches with respectful craft.

Mother stands restlessly by,
The cheque-book in her bag,
(And I know, without being told,
There's a world enlisting him
That hasn't a place for me.

O.K. I'll make my own).

Janus

I am the two-headed anniversary god,
Lord of the Lupercal and the Letts diary.
I have a head for figures.

My clocks are the moon and sun,
My almanac the zodiac. The ticktock seasons,
The hushabye seas are under my thumb.

From All Saints to All Souls I celebrate
The *da capo* year. My emblems are albums,
The bride's mother's orchid corsage, the dark cortège.

Master of the silent passacaglia
Of the future, I observe the dancers,
But never teach them the step.

I am the birthday prescience
Who knows the obituary, the tombstone's arithmetic.
Not telling is my present.

I monitor love through its mutations
From paper to ruby. I am archivist
Of the last divorce and the first kiss.

I am director of the forgotten fiesta.
I know why men at Bacup black their faces;
Who horned at Abbots Bromley tread the Mazes.

I am the future's overseer, the past's master.
See all, know all, speak not.
I am the two-faced god.

Resuscitation Team

Arrives like a jinn, instantly,
Equipped with beards, white coats, its own smell,
And armfuls of metal and rubber.

Deploys promptly round the quiet bed
With horseplay and howls of laughter.
We, who are used to life, are surprised

At this larky resurrection. Runs
Through its box of tricks, prick, poke and biff,
While we watch, amazed. The indifferent patient

Is not amused, but carries little weight,
Being stripped and fumbled
By so many rugger-players. My first corpse,

If she is a corpse, lies there showing
Too much breast and leg. The team
Rowdily throws up the sponge, demands soap and water,

Leaves at the double. One of us,
Uncertainly, rearranges the night-dress.
Is it professional to observe the proprieties

Now of her who leaves privately
Wheeled past closed doors, her face
Still in the rictus of victory?

What About Jerusalem?

'Would to God that all the Lord's people were prophets.' (Numbers,
11.29)

Wallflowers in your garden are stubbornly rooted,
Heeled in by you. Your magnolia sprouts fierce black buds.

In Sheffield and Gloucestershire, babies you drew into light
Flower and grow upright. A knack of giving life.

(I know 'em all, you'd swagger. *At least, their mothers I do.)*
They won't forget you, pain-killer, comforter.

Now you lie here in the chapel in pale wood,
White and yellow mortal flowers, and we sing

Jerusalem tentatively, waiting for you to pop up and exclaim
You've left out the feeling. So we have. I don't want to feel,

Gwen, that you've ended anything. *I will not cease,* we drone.
We haven't even started in the Great-heart way you did,

Who challenged geriatric consultants, hauled your friend
Out of dementia, brought her home to live.

Dear Gwen, who made the worst coffee I've ever tried
Not to drink, who never remembered a name

(You I mean! Whatnot!), who told explicit obstetric stories
Loudly, embarrassingly, in public rooms,

Who loved fast cars *(They pull in the birds)*
To my priggish disapproval; whose driving was known to the police.

I argued more with you than with anyone ever,
Though I'd seen you wink as you started to wind me up.

Is this all? Has that relentlessly
Self-educated mind at last run out of steam?

And such a little coffin. There's some trick here.
What about Jerusalem? You haven't ceased, have you?

Elaine Feinstein

Living Room

How can we make friends before one of us dies
if you quarrel with two fingers in your ears,
like a child? Things won't come out right now.
You think I don't love you. I won't argue.
Your angry sadness stings me into tears.
I think of your old mac, smelling of chemicals,
leant against long ago in the 'Everyman' queue,

when you offered me those tender early
films that made our lips tremble, or else
the forgiven boy in the forest of Ravel's opera,
more touching to me than your verbal
skills or passion for the genius of gesture
in crayon, mime, *commedia del arte.*
It's love we miss, and cannot bear to lose.

I know you would much prefer I choose
intelligence to prize, but that has
always had its down side, your words
so often cut me down to size, I wonder
if some accident removed me first, whether
my writing days would count as evidence
that in my loss was little real to miss.

The likeliest end is that the bay tree left
to my attention, withers on the window sill,
and moths lay eggs in the lentils, while
still hurt by memories of you as gentle, I'll
look into a monitor for comfort, and cry
aloud at night in the hope somewhere
your lonely spirit might hang on and care.

Against Winter

His kiss a bristling
beard in my ear, at 83:
'aren't you afraid of
dying?' I asked him (on his knee),
who shall excell his shrug for answer?

and yet was it long after,
senile, he lived in our front room,
once I had to
hold a potty out for him, his
penis was pink and clean as a child

and what he remembered of
Odessa and the Europe he walked through
was gone like the language I
never learned to speak, that
gave him resistance,

and his own sense of
favour (failed
rabbi, carpenter,
farmer in
Montreal)

and now I think
how the smell of
peppermint in his yellow
handkerchieves and the
snuff marks under his nose

were another part of it:
his sloven grace
(stronger than abstinence) that
was the source of his
undisciplined stamina.

Getting Older

The first surprise: I like it.
Whatever happens now, some things
that used to terrify have not:

I didn't die young, for instance. Or lose
my only love. My three children
never had to run away from anyone.

Don't tell me this gratitude is complacent.
We all approach the edge of the same blackness
which for me is silent.

Knowing as much sharpens
my delight in January freesia,
hot coffee, winter sunlight. So we say

as we lie close on some gentle occasion:
every day won from such
darkness is a celebration.

Home

Where is that I wonder?
Is it the book-packed house we plan to sell
with the pale green room above the river,
the shelves of icons, agate, Eilat stone
the Kathe Kollwitz and the Samuel Palmer?

Or my huge childhood house
oak-floored, the rugs of autumn colours, slabs of coal
in an open hearth, high-windowed rooms,
outside, the sunken garden, lavender, herbs
and trees of Victoria plum.

Last night I dreamed of
my dead father, white-faced, papery-skinned
and frailer than he died. I asked him:
- Doesn't all this belong to us? He shook his head,
bewildered. I was disappointed,

but though I woke with salt on my lips then
and a hoarse throat, somewhere between
the ocean and the desert, in an immense
Mexico of the spirit, I remembered
with joy and love my other ties of blood.

Kate Foley

Tall Foreign Doctor

She leans down from her gaunt height,
a crane in whose bill
storytellers have put kind words.

'Little women' she says
and their dark, slight bodies open.
Their vaginas are like torn flowers
to her hummingbird stitches.

Her foreign words clatter
like smooth stones.
Picked up
and dropped one by one,
each makes a small splash
in ears silted up
with fear and pain.

'It'll hurt
but you'll soon be better,
you'll go home in a new dress,
you'll marry again, have a live baby -
but remember - when your baby
starts walking inside you, you walk -
to the hospital.'

Intimate as a scalpel
she first cuts into their frightened hearts,
lifts out panic, heavy as a tired child,
and lays it down,
stitches up their courage,
tall as a tree with shade.

Dark, delicate, scared,
small women
take fierce, giant steps over the harsh plateau
to clean sheets and a painful cure.

Easy to be a tree-like foreign doctor
bending down a long way
to peer at their child-ripped bodies.
But she won't stay foreign.

She wants with passion
like a rush of blood to her freckles
to speak as they do,
like a chuckle of water,
mouth to mouth, equal
and her bending to be
landscape, like the crane's.

Fox on the Stairs

Feral as the sun's chestnut stain,
slipping like ruby glass,
fox leaves her spoor on every tread,
gilt spraints down each riser.

She wants me to follow,
though I can't catch her,
past the blazing pale of the bannisters,
onto the landing's gilded and distressed field.

Wild as best blue milk, fox milk,
sharp as dextrose spiking my blood,
she wants me crazy, bright teeth fastened
in my heart with a wilderness clasp.

No emblem, she trots, tongue lolling,
up the vertebral column of the house,
past each blue eyelid shuttered room,
bright as a needle through folded shadow.

Her musk paints the air impasto
and I will never bleach it clean
or feel the house like a newly
bathed domestic animal, settle.

Here's the House, where's the Steeple?

How do I know your hands
tell me the truth? Because
mine cannot lie.

Stripped of carefulness
in the strong disinfectant of truth
they're naked, no longer ready

for easy, familiar gestures,
for wooing or soothing
when they should fall silent in my lap.

When your hand crept cold,
sweaty, trembling, into mine,
no words were said,

but mine, trembling back,
confirmed the invitation.
Your hands are limber,

nimble, good at making
gothic steeples,
while mine make roman arches.

But used to the last resource
of touch, each neuron fired,
fingers speaking in tongues,

our hands lie, resting quietly
after the work of love,
in the earned interlace of silence.

The Only Ghost

Breath finds you out
when you hide.
Hung in its swung moment of poise
like the tide,
it waits
till you plunge.

You can't fool breath,
it searches out
your flaccid veins,
forces them wide
like mussels in the pan.

Breath is a harsh cleanser.
It hurtles birds through space
on their hollow bones,
jets oxygen
to scavenge your dumb blood
till your nerves blaze
and your heart creaks.

It is astringent,
as unlike chlorophyll
as high octane fuel,
as the grassy breath of cows
to the stinking wind
of our hungers.

But once, like a frog
in a blue bubble
on the pond's bottom
we were held
in the caul of our mother's breath,

and now as breath
is shared
in the cup of our mouths,
or it leaves
like a small wave turning over,
we know it is
our one true,
our only ghost.

Wendy French

On the Sunny Side

                    of South Street
Mr Wong's offering his happy hour
an hour early and though your stomach's flat
as a punctured tyre you've got money.

You walk past inflated plastic girls
lit in neon sex shops. Half eaten soap
and torn up photos fill your bag
as you poke with a skeletal umbrella,
fighting someone else's air.

Trying to persuade you to come back
to the ward I follow but free will,
you say, won't come until you're dead,
you're Hansel and Gretl,

and I'm the mother witch squeezing
the last drops of milk out of my breast.
Was it worth it? You scream at me now,
skirt hitched round your bottom,
boobs thin and wasted. I rehearse

so many phrases but I know the words
that I'll throw down to let you eat
the words you'll say when the storm
lights up the pavement.

Katherine Frost

Our Son Has Two Mothers

It's the story he's been hearing
since he was small enough
to slot into my lap like the last piece of the jigsaw,
his little hard tail nudging my groin
to be let back in.
We'd be crouched the way we are now
to his child's atlas, where England's
nothing much, South America
a yokeyellow kite
elbowing the upstreams.
Heads bowed, my frayed beech to his
dense black - to the petrol violet
depth of it that owes nothing
to English halftones,
between an armadillo and a palm
we'd make a place
for where he began:
'We'll go,' I'd say, 'all of us.
When you're older.' 'Soon'.

But today, he's telling it, and just like that I see
I'm not there.
Not there as his blunt plane pants after the sun
a day, a night, another day,
not there when he stumbles out
to aquarium heat and shabby grass, suddenly
nowhere he's ever dreamed of,
while all the gaps between the snapshots
wheel up to flap round him
like huge unwelcome birds.

Not there either when at last he can run,
arms outstretched, down the
crooked path between shacks
that cling to the river,
shedding as he goes his socks,

his Doc Marten boots, his
Fireman Sam shirt;
                    and shrinking
to smaller than he is now, growing thin,
as the children were that I remember
and he doesn't, outside shacks
just like these,
running to the mother he'll know,
though he's seen her just once
when he pushed out of her.

There's a pause with arms wrapped round each other,
the young woman with her tiny adorer,
before they lean back
from the waist to let each other see
how they do fit, what a match they are,
the dulce de leche skin-tones blending -

at a distance you hardly
can tell just where
his narrow wrist becomes hers.

Cynthia Fuller

Dream Fish

The fish swam through her dreams again,
its soft gape shining with needles,
its evil eye. There will be no
twisting arc of death today, she said,
no slippery writhing after breath.
I have beached the red boat safe
from the curl of the wave's lip.
How he sneered. As if dreams should rule,
or women's fears. He took his boat out.
From the cottage on the cliff she watched.
She saw him standing, his net ballooning
with small quick fish; she saw her own boat
trim and dry; malevolent as broken faith
she saw the dream fish surfacing.

Anne-Marie Fyfe

Our House

I come home late to find
my key won't turn in the lock.
Murmurs drift from rooms.
Through the letterbox a child's bike,
a woman's coat on the banister. Beige.
No one answers our door
its scarlet gloss dull now.
I walk up my neighbour's path,
relief as she opens the door.
But she shifts when I say
I'm from next door. No. Some mistake.
The next-doors are long gone,
no word if they'll ever be back.
People inside? No. Never.
She's not heard a pin drop behind
those walls.
           When I get back
to our red door they're switching
off lamps, climbing stairs.
Our bedroom is the last to go.

Katherine Gallagher

Poem for a Shallot

I am fooled.
You insist on the secret of skins -
how perfectly each wraps you.

You compartmentalize,
I don't know how.
I can peel you back to nothing.

I hunt for what isn't there -
layer upon layer -
down to your cagey heart.

When I try to get away
you've snuck into my breath, eyes,
making me cry

into my hands.

Hunger

She is thinking of the last time he touched her -
how he stroked her, said she was losing weight

as if it represented a country they had to get to, as if
the fat could curl back to the bone like years undone.

And she saw they stood between their shadows and the wolf
who howls for them in the night.

Jet Lag

I didn't go round the world. It went around me
crossing time zones in my sealed-off balloon,

following inflight-arrows across Europe,
Asia, Australia. Don't ask what day it is -

my body clock ticks in those concertinaed
intervals between borders and continents,

oceans urging them forward.
I can't find sleep. Instead I have birds

crisscrossing the lanes of my head.
They saw my airship slip by and me peering

through a window, setting my watch
by the stars. I'll catch up with this shaky life,

wrap it around me like a quick nap.
Leonardo put such problems on hold

with his *ornithopter*, needing wings
to flap before it could move.

So much for all that sky-gazing,
wanting to get off the ground.

Now I'll just sleep on possibilities.
I'm still thirty thousand feet up,

nudging clouds like a sunset, the day
slipping through my fingers.

A Visit to the War Memorial, Canberra

We have scratched their names
on the national bronze

cradled them
in a dark photograph

We have collected their medals
ranked them behind glass

carried their relics
through mirages and warnings

We have taken their legends
the words that couldn't halt

the backdrop-massacres
and tainted forests

We have heard dry laughter
breaking their silences

as they kept marching
despite their chagrin

bagging their history
in the tally of requiems

whispering their names
over and over

in halls of recognition
where feet crunch on boards

and conversations
breed silences

Pamela Gillilan

Country Living, 1955

It was different when he played in London.
Now he comes home heavier by pounds,
wet soil impacted into cloth and skin,
face earthed and sweaty. It was different

in London, with a warm plunge after.
The steam smoothed, softened him,
made him shine - that and the post mortem
with mates in the bar. Now he washes

bit by bit in the kitchen, stove-heated water
drawn from the well, laborious pailfuls.
His boots aren't dry all season; dubbiny, soggy,
they wait out each week until Saturday's

emergence, the brushing away of mildew's frosting.
He laces them on, after socks and pads and socks,
and clatters up the village hill in kit
that still smells of effort and wormcasts.

I prepare, as if awaiting a midwife,
the bowls of hot water that will wash him
incompletely clean - though cleaner than I,
in the guilt of my grudging. For him

the afternoon escape to air and speed;
dull indoor tasks for me. The black
reluctant coalstove glowers, the baby's
wrapped hunger simmers in the pram

and I have too little trust or clarity,
struggling against the moment's bonds,
though of themselves they'll fall; and he,
whom indeed I love, won't make old bones.

August

(for C.S.)

Riding around the lanes
we stopped at dusk by a field gate,
wheeled our bikes through, leant them
against the hawthorn hedge.

The ground was set hard into the ruts
of old rains, but we found
a smoother slope to lie on.
Well, passion might have built

except that, the sky's blue darkening,
we turned to a new brightness growing
along the meadow's edge; and then
the rising of a vast, round moon.

Town moons had never
been so brilliant, seemed so near,
shed down such ripened light,
nor called out such crowd.

Whole families ran, scampering
and tumbling across the grass.
Bold in their play they rushed
so close to where we lay

we almost saw each single hair, each
twitching nose, each jet-bead eye,
each sensitive long ear - tonight
oblivious of threat. We watched

until, limbs stiff, we had to move.
Under that sailing lamp
we walked our bikes in silence,
towards our separate beds.

Ann Gray

Solace

Sometimes a day that started badly
can end with geese -

a lake of heads and necks, a sound
so like young dogs, or donkeys, calling

from one distant yard to another
across a stretch of land where no-one

cares what day it is, except the month
is hot and somehow drowsy. Wasps

sing of apples rotting in the grass.
There is a steadfastness about the purple

of the heather, the fat acorns,
the way the greens move imperceptibly

closer to other colours. There is no
hurry anywhere, not even in the rushing

of the water, and the clouds
have fallen into any shape you want them.

Cathy Grindrod

Dispossessed

Switch off the computer,
face the blank screen:
remove the plug, the chip.
Leave my desk as it once was.

Let me go to the place I call home.
I shall walk there, alone.
Take all I own, remove it.
Leave floorboards, dust, light.
Let the flames lick, burn bright.

All those I love, kiss once,
with one palm wipe minds clean.

I will take off my own clothes;
make a small pile; necklace;
rings; this ring,
drop. Let it lie,
become grey ash when fires die.

Last of all my shoes,
heel, lace, sole and tongue remove.

I will go to a place I choose,
to flowers no man grew;
an opening to trees,
grass, kind night.
Small scurryings only.

Think only then of who I am.
Tell it to the stars.

Lucy Hamilton

Rings *i.m. John Plowright*

A tree is thick - or thin -
      skinned, its sap
carries sugar
      to leaves, feeds
new cells, infuses
      roots with energy

and the cambium -
      almost invisible -
is as oxygen to blood:
      a tree's power
to live is in this
      cell-thick film.

I remember
      when a child,
you showed me how to read
      a tree's mind,
understand rings' secrets -
      like ripples

radiating from flint
      skimmed on water
reveal a lone man's
      arc of back,
swing of arm - inner
      stillness.

The heartwood is
      the dead centre,
trees' strength, rigidity;
      if air reaches
the heart it decays,
      makes hollow.

But no-one knows
      how it bends
its dead heart
      to reach the light
or why drilling for
      poems is filling holes.

Diana Hendry

In Defence of Pianos

(for Ben Kernighan)

In every alien place you find a piano -
schools, hospitals, prisons, asylums,
the homes of friends, your own front room.
Either they have been there forever
with a squeaky pedal and a dud B flat
or they breech-birth a window
and can't get back.

They should be extinct, these stranded uprights
lost in an iron-mongery moonlight
of genteel dust. The grand ones, got up
like mermaids in ebony velvet, bare
the awful symmetry of their jaws
in crocodile smiles
across the Albert Hall.

My Grös and Kallman, Berlin hausfrau, importantly
panelled and touched-up with brass, has two
timing pendulums engraved on her heart.
Her dreaming feet never touch the floor
and despite her homely Song-Book looks
she'll still flannel her hammers
with Wolfgang or Joseph.

O my frog-prince of furniture, I write
in your defence, having heard it said
that the lion's roar matches the desert,
the elephant's blare breaches the dark,
the bear can snarl at winter and snow
but man has only
a rented piano -

It is not widely known how far through the dark
of a night a piano can go, nor how

it can take to the streets in summer flight
so that hearing it ragging the silence you'd think
that man rented a forest to make a piano,
its falling pine needles
notes from home.

The Lace Makers

(for Grace Brinkley)

They turn inward, to the dark of their doorways,
patient as porous rocks to soak up all shadow.
Only then, when they've bodily blotted up darkness
and each is as shadow-full as a fountain pen with ink,
can a few lines of White Mountain lace slip
like poesy's oozy gum, from their hooks and fingers.

The thread they use - drawn from a basketed spool
at their feet - might well be that which Theseus used
fumbling back from the gloom. Their crochet hooks
work like the mind making patterns of meaning. Their lace
they learnt as children watching foam and sea-spray
hem the beach. Now outside dark Venetian shops their cloths

dangle on poles and dazzle the tourists we've all become
with such a blinding white it's as if death itself
has been washed and sunned and the table laid for wine
and the bed for love and on each sheet and spread
there's lace to compensate for all that's rough on us,
that wounds the flesh with loss - of youth, or hope, or health.

Phoebe Hesketh

Mary

Mary under the hawthorn
sat waiting
listening
watching worlds outside her ring of leaves
flying feet folded as birds
hands holding stillness.

Shadows shrank into her green tent
bunched under noonday sun.
Not a leaf, not a wing brushed the air
and the rushing world grew still as an egg -
only Mary of the cupped hands
heard the song under the shell.

Gone Away

When we thought him near
he was away
far side of the hill.
While in thickets we tore him apart,
ate him alive, flung his heart to the dogs,
he eluded us still.

Gone-away fox -
no hounds will bring him back;
melted in distance he runs
through Sirius, Orion.
The hungry pack
trails him in vain; suns
have gone down on his blood.

His breath is autumn mist;
yellowing leaves
glint with his topaz look.
Gone away, away, away -
he is over the brook.

Preparing to Leave

Attics cleared; shelves and drawers emptied;
Love-letters burned and memory purged,
I knew we had always been
Preparing to leave.
Those wedding-groups, snaps of childhood,
Babyhood, parents - back, back
To the unremembered, thrust
Deep into the dustbin.
The lid clashes louder than the Bible
That life is grass;
Possessions rust;
And man a moment of hope
From centuries' dust.

I walk out into wet fields of spring;
Plovers are circling,
Crying to the rain and the trees,
Calling their young from empty nests -
Even these
Are pulled away on the swirl and heave
Of the wind.
All things that live are preparing to leave.

After Ecclesiastes

The day of death is better than the day of one's birth.

And the end of a party is better than the beginning.
Quietness gathers the voices and laughter
into one cup -
we drink peace.

Crumpled cushions are smoothed as our souls
and silence comes into the room
like a stranger bearing gifts
we had not imagined,
could not have known
without such comings
and such departures.

Selima Hill

I Am Hers and She Is Mine

When I was young I knitted flocks of sheep.
I kept them like an army on the landing,
drilled to watch her door, and storm her room,
reporting back on everything they saw.
And in the winter as the days drew in
I knitted every sheep a little cardigan
to keep them warm at night while they waited.
They waited. But she never came back.
She went away to be a grown woman.
Our partnership however gathered strength.
We spent our lives perfecting being enemies
and now it's automatic: I am hers
and she - whom now I only meet in dreams,
with painted face and dogs on chains - is mine.

The Fish Hospital

It's all very well you
shouting at me like that
and trying to get me to answer
your endless questions
but what you don't seem to realise is
that my head -
just as I thought it couldn't be
stretched so tight,
and feel so cold,
and creak like ice,
one minute longer -
has turned itself
into a goldfish-bowl.
I have to use all my powers of concentration
to keep balanced,
and keep quiet,
for the sake of the fish
that squirm about at the bottom
in not enough water

like lips and tongues
being buried alive under snow,
that are struggling to cry,
but they can't,
they're not formed properly,
while outside in the fields
windswept nurses,
standing in the snow
in their dressing-gowns,
have finally given up waving
they're so cold.

Liz Houghton

Persian Lamb

Mother is knitting: plain, purl, in, out.
In her wardrobe Persian lamb hangs in polythene.
Does she know about Mr. Gregory: hanging in his garage?
Was it because I stole the marbles?
Moths hang inside the new glass shade.
I remember the lamb's lining on my skin,
the night I danced naked in the mirror.
How long did you hang there Mr. Gregory?
Questions without answers.
You won't see the coronation on somebody's TV
with curtains drawn in the day.
We've a new Queen now in nineteen-fifty-three.
It's a new Elizabethan age, but your shop
is: *Closed for an indefinite period.*
Mother doesn't know I'm a thief and a murderer,
doesn't know I touched the lamb, slid it
from the slippery hanger, let it swish round my feet,
pressed my nose in its shiny wool. Why did they kill it?
Who can I ask? Plain, purl.
Questions without answers.
What would happen if she knew I'd touched her lamb,
rolled the marbles between my hot palms,
cried over squirming colours trapped in glass.
I'm sorry Mr. Gregory, do you feel better, now you are dead?

Sue Hubbard

Assimilation

I never knew whether to say Amen.
In the vaulted hall silent girls dipped
rosy profiles into dust-freckled sunlight

while I stood dumb-lipped trapped by
the trinity of longing, fear, propriety,
the word stillborn in my throat.

Alone at thirteen in shadows of Dresden
blue, I bore the guilt of history, somehow
felt the weight of censure for what they'd done.

Head bowed consulting the diamond perforations on
regulation shoes, burnt ashes branded my tongue
with the double stigmata: unbeliever, hypocrite.

I did not know where I'd come from but guessed
at their journey through the snowflecked storms
of some Lithuanian December night

creeping through purple larch and spruce to flee
the zealous pogroms and their indignant Slavic rage.
Yet I've never tasted the sweet wine of Kiddush.

Beyond the stained-glass windows and the Annunciation
English playing fields stretched printed
with tramlines, the watermarks of fair play.

In the back of the cupboard in my father's study
a tarnished silver samovar lay in waiting for
tall glasses, lemon and a scoop of Russian tea.

Elizabeth Jennings

Tribute

Sometimes the tall poem leans across the page
And the whole world seems near, a simple thing.
Then all the arts of mind and hand engage
To make the shadow tangible. O white
As silence is the page where words shall sing
And all the shadows be drawn into light.

And no one else is necessary then.
The poem is enough that joins me to
The world that seems too far to grasp at when
Images fail and words are gabbled speech:
At those times clarity appears in you,
Your mind holds meanings that my mind can reach.

Are you remote, then, when words play their part
With a fine arrogance within the poem?
Will the words keep all else outside my heart,
Even you, my test of life and gauge?
No, for you are that place where poems find room,
The tall abundant shadow on my page.

Song for a Birth or a Death

Last night I saw the savage world
And heard the blood beat up the stair;
The fox's bark, the owl's shrewd pounce,
The crying creatures - all were there,
And men in bed with love and fear.

The slit moon only emphasised
How blood must flow and teeth must grip.
What does the calm light understand,
The light which draws the tide and ship
And drags the owl upon its prey
And human creatures lip to lip?

Last night I watched how pleasure must
Leap from disaster with its will:
The fox's fear, the watch-dog's lust
Know that all matings mean a kill;
And human creatures kissed in trust
Feel the blood throb to death until

The seed is struck, the pleasure's done,
The birds are thronging in the air;
The moon gives way to widespread sun.
Yes but the pain still crouches where
The young fox and the child are trapped
And cries of love are cries of fear.

The Island

All travellers escape the mainland here.
The same geology torn from the stretch
Of hostile homelands is a head of calm,
And the same sea that pounds a foreign beach
Turns strangers here familiar, looses them
Kindly as pebbles shuffled up the shore.

Each brings an island in his heart to square
With what he finds, and all is something strange
But most expected. In this innocent air
Thoughts can assume a meaning, island strength
Is outward, inward, each man measures it,
Unrolls his happiness a shining length.

And this awareness grows upon itself,
Fastens on minds, is forward, backward, here.
The island focuses escape and free
Men on the shore are also islands, steer
Self to knowledge of self in the calm sea,
Seekers who are their own discovery.

Song at the Beginning of Autumn

Now watch this autumn that arrives
In smells. All looks like summer still;
Colours are quite unchanged, the air
On green and white serenely thrives.
Heavy the trees with growth and full
The fields. Flowers flourish everywhere.

Proust who collected time within
A child's cake would understand
The ambiguity of this -
Summer still raging while a thin
Column of smoke stirs from the land
Proving that autumn gropes for us.

But every season is a kind
Of rich nostalgia. We give names -
Autumn and summer, winter, spring -
As though to unfasten from the mind
Our moods and give them outward forms.
We want the certain, solid thing.

But I am carried back against
My will into a childhood where
Autumn is bonfires, marbles, smoke;
I lean against my window fenced
From evocations in the air.
When I said autumn, autumn broke.

Sylvia Kantaris

Some Untidy Spot

(in memory of Meryon)

Tragedies happen anyhow, in corners, when other people
are working or just walking dully along,
as Auden said, thinking of Brueghel's Icarus
who fell into the water in the space between
two glances, and then into the painting, then the poem,
as if the whole Aegean was not wide enough
to hold the impact of the moment of his death.
But this poem is about your son
who was too young to fly like Icarus
and simply walked behind you on an ordinary path
along an ordinary river's edge
then wasn't on the path when you looked back.
So all the lives he might have lived slipped out of him
in ripples and were gone, to all appearances,
yet grow in circles which are not contained
by any accidental river bank, or even
by the confines of your heart which held him
firmly, safe behind great dykes of love,
but couldn't ring the moment or the one untidy spot.

O Little Star

I only had to wet my knickers twice -
first time during prayers in the infants' class.
'Fold hands, bow heads, close eyes and now repeat:
Our Father ...' ('The radiator's leaking,'
Janet whispered. 'It's me,' I whispered back.)
The second time, appointed as the Angel due to
long blonde hair (and also to fortify my ego)
I stood up on a chair to have my wings attached.
All in white, my halo glittering, I peed again
and had to be rushed out, detinselled and disgraced.
Ann played the part instead. I was half glad.
The teacher cast herself as the Voice of God.

After school, I manned the garden gate
and lifted my skirt when people passed.
'Knickers!' I hissed, then ran and hid.
'Your daughter needs a board strapped to her back
to keep it straight,' the teacher told my mother
after I'd exposed my navy knickers at her.
So off I went to school with a plank to bear
(like Jesus, I fondly told myself). And at
the Easter service I was like the Lamb, our Saviour,
and didn't wet my knickers. I just bleated
soulfully about the cross I suffered,
and got a gold star for my good behaviour.

Next nativity, *I* played God-the-Father
(invisible, off-stage, but what the hell).
I said, 'Just say exactly what I tell thee Gabriel.'

Martha Kapos

Fishing in an Old Wound

Fished in an old wound,
The soft pond of repose;
Nothing nibbled my line,
Not even the minnows came.
Theodore Roethke

Fishing in an old wound
where, for all I know, I am
the fish, mouth airy as a cave,
waiting vertical and still in the dark.

Exactly in the center is the red hook
baited with succinct meat.
Fluttering mouth caught on the long
illusion, I suck hope against hope.

Whose red badge do I trail home,
nodding, an idiot in my skin,
tilted as a fish travelling on its side
out of true? The way back is streaked

with red. There I am again and again
throwing the trawling line in the wound.
It keeps flapping open

like brilliantly white curtains
blowing from an upstairs window,
like a baby held in the air,
as though the four drowned walls

of the kitchen boasted a high-tide mark,
as though the ceiling had forgotten its
predictable height. Is it enough?

The stiff chairs improvise at the table;
a skin of milk wrinkles on the cup.
Clouds blow over, stunted
shadows moving under an even light.

Origin of the Sexes According to Aristophanes

Our simplicity of feeling was an explosion.
Fireworks - especially Catherine wheels
circled the sky. We spun out
head-over-heels an elated shower
of lights. We had at least two heads,
four arms and legs, and several tongues.
Spikes grew from the fingers of our
unclenched hands; a thousand forms burst
with a deafening report from our beating
hearts. Our high voices rolled
the length of the horizon for hours on end
without falling. We were blue touch-paper,
rings of hung mist, red-haloed chisel-points
in the dark. Shooting stars had nothing on our
full speed, forced landings in mid-air,
our perfect incendiary curves.
Our ascent to heaven would surely
take place at any moment; and the rest
of the world backed away, for who
can embrace a fire? 'This perfection must stop!'
A god stepped in. The swift parting slice
of an axe. Since then the lights have dimmed,
and we must hop about the earth on two legs.

Judith Kazantzis

A Photograph Seen When I Was Twelve

There were women of all ages
their shoulders bunched forward,
running before guards with pistols,
dogs, long coats with high collars.

- You know now, so why say more?

One hand thrown across her breasts,
the other thrown across her mound of Venus,
dark-haired, thick like the dishevelled
dark hair round her staring face.

I can't forget these Venuses of the earth,
fat, flabby, crouching before blows.

Standing hidden behind a thick pine trunk,
smelling its resin in the cold,
my nose pressed to the barbed wire,
blobs of snow falling without lightness,
licking the high collar of my dirty mac.

I opened the book and looked at the picture,
closed it in shame, opened it, closed it,
opened it, stared at the women,
not millions, there were ten of them

who ran in the perishing cold
beyond the barbed wire and the pine trunk
(into which I pressed myself with disbelief).
They ran on out of my line of vision,
they were prodded beyond.

I left their naked bodies and stared
at their faces, and, running, their eyes
eyed me back; the small round woman
in front, she had wavy ragged hair

and broad cheeks, the next was slender
with arched nose - The prints were very bad.

Yet I insisted, huddling my piled clothing
behind the pine tree and the barbed wire,
I know her, I shouted, caught on hooks,
she works behind the till in the store,
curtly dealing out change as she says -

how's the family; and the one with
the fine bones is my history teacher
whose calm desire to be objective,
to wait carefully for the examination results
of history, I argue with passionately.

Her fine dark blonde hair is wrenched out,
everything gone. I couldn't burst out, turn,
nothing and no one. Not I, no one,
to rip the guards out cold
from their barbed wire costumes.

Only that since then at the border
I have stood naked, and look forever
at these hardly discernible women's faces,
who were the queens of their bodies
until the final day, and shall be;
though they were taken from themselves.

For Mahesh, Deported

For reasons to do with the paper
unstamped, the wrong stamp,
for reasons to do with your skin,

the drawn lines across your forehead,
the tired sails of your eyelids,
your hands disposing

the waste of other sumptuous lives,
the palms cracked and stamped with
the hot water - Your hands

when you took hold of mine quickly
and said goodbye, were too cold,
small, too cold, dry, no matter

how you smiled and bossed me around -
goodbye! As if it was your house,
that place, and you were showing me out.

Mimi Khalvati

The Piano

You have found your digital metronome.
Where, you didn't say. I have never said,
or always said in so many words, how a piano
is nothing to the weight I bear. Your throat
so soft, feet bare, where you played the violin
in pyjamas, and the black and white cat whose instinct
for camouflage would draw him to the stool
when we weren't there - you didn't find it there.

Downstairs. On the ground floor of our lives.
Nor, in a flat whose floors walk into trees,
was it anywhere near the old metronome,
broken, mechanical, you'd repositioned;
flung aside with your oval clock I rescued,
reassembled, dismissed the missing sliver
of glass no-one'll notice. The piano tuner
didn't steal it then. - Just as well.

A body is a thing of dread. A thing
of guilt. Desire and dream. Something
to purge with percussion. How rare it is
to merge with, to have your own organs sing
through another's. See, it has taken blindness
from your touch, the grime you took from newsprint,
down escalator rails. Milk will revive
its ivory. It must be cared for in silence.

And even a piano must have water. Be
listened to for the precise pitch of health.
How it hurts you. Hurts where you have already
hurt yourself. It is in step. I will take
the shawl it has worn so long nothing short
of washing will remove its folds and dents.
I don't want to remove them. Such a worn-in
fit is rare. I am cold. I'm cold, Tom, play.

Villanelle

No one is there for you. Don't call, don't cry.
No one is in. No flurry in the air.
Outside your room are floors and doors and sky.

Clocks speeded, slowed, not for you to question why,
Tick on. Trust them. Be good, behave. Don't stare.
No one is there for you. Don't call, don't cry.

Cries have their echoes, echoes only fly
Back to their pillows, flocking back from where
Outside your room are floors and doors and sky.

Imagine daylight. Daylight doesn't lie.
Fool with your shadows. Tell you nothing's there,
No one is there for you. Don't call, don't cry.

But daylight doesn't last. Today's came by
To teach you the dimensions of despair.
Outside your room are floors and doors and sky.

Learn, when in turn they turn to you, to sigh
And say: 'You're right, I know, life isn't fair.'
No one is there for you. Don't call, don't cry.
Outside your room are floors and doors and sky.

Middle Age

There are those who are radiant confronting
death in cornflower blues and violets.
There are roofs that kneel to large shapes of sun
submissively as cows to the sky's gait.
I protect myself from happiness, rooting
into the search for it, mourning its youth,
though it's the lesser courage that admits
to unhappiness, to gladness, the greater.
What did we vow we'd be in middle age? -
young of course. Immortal. Assuming process
reversible by that effort of will

only gods possess, protean, promethean.
Knowing we'd die but not knowing how tired
we'd get, even of loving, how we'd fear
emotion. No one tells us. How we'd get
our second wind from death and even then
only those who are charmed, transformed by grace
we think a miracle - who knows what strength
it takes, who only sees those blue eyes bluer,
who only sees apparel. No one tells us
about middle age. Forget teeth, sight, hearing,
what about the heart? You'd think it a dumb
organ, stones in its well, a clobbered clock
not knowing moments from minutes, stone itself.
I tell my heart to move, it doesn't. Look,
I say, what do you like out there, tail feathers?
It looks but doesn't see, sees but can't name.
It's middle-aged. I think of Keats and wonder
how one so young could feel it rich to die
till I remember illness, pain. And though
here I am healthy, knowing pain will pass,
from where I am I catch the drift of it -
a wind that blows the other way. Or rather,
doesn't blow but being ever more easeful,
makes me see, as if in a glassy surface,
fingers dragged in the shallows of its wake.

Writing Letters

After chapel on Sundays we wrote letters.
Ruling pencil lines on airmails. Addresses
on front and back often bearing the same name,
same initial even, for in some countries
they don't bother to draw fine lines between
family members with an alphabet.

Those who remembered their first alphabet
covered the page in reams of squiggly letters
while those who didn't envied them. Between
them was the fine line of having addresses
that spelt home, home having the ring of countries
still warm on the tongue, still ringing with their name,

and having addresses gone cold as a name
no one could pronounce in an alphabet
with no *k-h*. Some of us left our countries
behind where we left our names. Wrote our letters
to figments of imagination: addresses
to darlings, dears, we tried to tell between,

guessing at norms, knowing the choice between
warmth and reserve would be made in the name
of loyalty. As we learnt our addresses
off by heart, the heart learnt an alphabet
of doors, squares, streets off streets, where children's letters
felt as foreign as ours from foreign countries.

Countries we revisited later; countries
we reclaimed, disowned again, caught between
two alphabets, the back and front of letters.
Street names change; change loyalties: a king's name
for a saint's. Even the heart's alphabet
needs realignment when the old addresses

sink under flyovers and new addresses
never make it into books where their countries
are taken as read. In an alphabet
of silence, dust, where the distance between
darling and dear is desert, where no name
is traced in the sand, no hand writes love letters,

none of my addresses can tell between
camp and home, neither of my countries name
this alphabet a cause for writing letters.

from: 'Entries on Light'

It is said
    God created a peacock of light
and placed him
    in front of a mirror.
In the presence
    of God, being so ashamed at his own
beauty, his own
    unutterable perfection, the peacock

broke out in a sweat.
    From the sweat of his nose, God created
the Angels.
    From the sweat of his face, the Throne, Footstool
Tablet of Forms, the Pen
    the heavens and what is in them.
From breast and back
    the Visited House, prophets, holy sites, etc.

From the sweat of his two feet
    God created, from east to west, the earth.
The sea is
    glistening peacock sweat.
Tarmac too.
    From sweat of the peacock's feet of pearl
comes my window view.
    Perhaps I am formed from a trembling

drop on his ankle.
    Cypress, sunflower, bicycle wheels
grass dried in heat
    to the colour of wheat, all, all are
peacock water, peacock dew
    shame and beauty, salt and light
God's peacock
    in his consciousness, walks over.

Lotte Kramer

Earthquake

'Please save my brother, he's still there' he said
Clutching his pen, wearing his pin-stripe suit,
Though dust and mortar stiffened him to lead.

The rubble falling around him and his head
Dizzy and bleeding. 'I'm an accountant,
Please save my brother, he's still there' he said.

It took six seconds for the earth to shed
Her mother image and destroy its root
When dust and mortar stiffened him to lead.

Too few can crawl to safety from their bed,
Escape the knock at dawn, the vicious boot.
'Please save my brother, he's still there' he said.

Pompeii choked. No time for wine and bread.
Vesuvius boiled and strangled every street.
The dust and mortar stiffened him to lead.

We walk away from craters, feel instead
Some kind of grief for one whose world is mute.
'Please save my brother, he's still there' he said
Though dust and mortar stiffened him to lead.

Cocoon

She says she can't remember anything
Of people, language, town; not even school
Where we were classmates. Her smile is frail
And hides behind her husband's hypnotising

Quietness. 'A Suffolk man' he beams,
And squares his tweedy frame against some
Unseen advocates who might still claim
An inch of her. She is content, it seems,

To lose her early childhood; he is near.
Protector or destroyer, it's his war.
He underwrites her willed amnesia,
Helps her to stifle terror, exile, fear.

She is cocooned, safe as an English wife,
Never to split that shell and crawl through love.

Bilingual

When you speak German
The Rhineland opens its watery gates,
Lets in strong currents of thought.
Sentences sit on shores teeming
With certainties. You cross bridges
To travel many lifetimes
Of a captive's continent.

When you speak English
The hesitant earth softens your vowels.
The sea - never far away - explores
Your words with liquid memory.
You are an apprentice again and skill
Is belief you can't quite master
In your adoptive island.

Myself, I'm unsure
In both languages. One, with mothering
Genes, at once close and foreign
After much unuse. Near in poetry.
The other, a constant love affair
Still unfulfilled, a warm
Shoulder to touch.

Gwyneth Lewis

Coconut Postcards

A Goan Honeymoon

I

Wrapped in the palm trees' parentheses
the peninsula sighs. The repeated Vs
rustle of rain to come, but not tonight...
One tree is everything to us - is food, is light,
shelter and matting, drunkenness and shade,
boat or a ladder. We use it shamelessly -
eating it, plaiting it, as though it were made
solely for us, and still it gives more.
It's rooted in loving and has no fear
of its own exhaustion. Note how its star
is an asterisk: something important is planted here.

II

'You can have all the one-night stands you want
with me once we're married.' Along the waterfront
bee-eaters squeal as they strip the air
of its writing of insects; seagulls pilfer
wrist-watch crabs from the clock of the sea
which tells us our time. Like a silver boat
the moon has set sail on the light that we
must take as our monument today,
for we've married each other's dying. We pay
the ferryman's fare as he poles his way
past porpoise rip-tides in the darkening bay.

III

Back in his Sanskrit childhood, when a pile of stones
was a god, the Contractor was never alone,
was pantheistic. Now his head's a Kali
fixed to the sway of an avenger's body
in a ruined temple - a pose he holds for the wife.
He refuses to swim because of jellyfish,

which disgust him. He has lived a life
of thrust, of direction, he is a man of spine,
despising drift. But he fears the sting
of the floating organ, whose transparent design
can kill him by willing nothing.

IV

Entombed on their towels, the honeymooners gleam . . .
Alabaster limbs and gothic dreams
keep waiters away, for they lie in state.
Burnished by unguents they concentrate
on just being, now that all their delights
are formal, official. So their smiles are fixed -
eyes closed to the wheeling Brahminy kites
above, to the life around them, to the dissolute
hibiscus tongues, to the siren's alarms
as a baby's found buried in a palm tree's roots,
re-born from the earth into fostering arms.

V

Palm number eight is a toddy-tapping tree,
is fortunate, owns a family
which tends to its every need. In return
it allows them to place a strategic urn
over its sweetly bleeding stem
so that Polycarp d'Souza's still
is full. All night the palm tree bleeds for them.
At noon, girls gather in its fertile shade,
striped like tigers, for their husbandry's
ferocious - best marriage a tree could have made
against its main enemy, gravity.

VI

By the shack a man wants to clean out my ears
and then massage me. In the end I concur
and settle my lug-hole so that he can reach
its whorls. He digs and suddenly the beach
is louder. He picks out detritus, wax and more -
out comes a string of my memories -

leaving me light in the midday roar
of sand grains crashing and singing crabs. I'm
relieved of all the rubbish I've ever heard,
re-tuned, a transistor that can hear the first time
the call of the heart's hidden weaver-bird.

VII

On the beach you can practise our history
and crawl, amphibian, up from the sea
then under umbrellas to be something cool
in shorts and dark glasses. Look quizzical
as the sea's empty metre sighs at the feet
of a palm that carries flowers, acorns, fruit
all the same moment. At dusk we're freed
from shape into colour. On an opal tide
we swim: skin opens into lilacs and far
below the tuna's silver shoots through my side.
I reach out my tongue and lick Africa.

VIII

This place, like paradise, is better than us
but accepts us graciously, puts us at ease
with love's broad tolerance, so kind
that it only condemns the begrudging mind,
which exiles itself. For the moment, my dear,
simplification's the name of the game.
Set me up slowly like a folding chair
in the sun and, serenely, let's look out together
at the scenery and common life
which bless us repeatedly in the insect stir
of a palm-frond husband with his sea-breeze wife.

Stone Walls

There is an art to seeing through walls.
Old Mícheál had it as he closed these miles

of Burren pasture. He was a man
whose straightness was in great demand

for he never saw gradient, but would build
right up a cliff face, aiming beyond

for the logical summit. He would place
two boulders together with such poise

that they'd mimic the line of a far-off spur,
rhyming with limestone, making being here

a matter of artistry. I've seen grown men
who scorn the wit of a well-placed dolmen

laugh at his corners, which made visible
the herringbone cast of his rhythmic soul,

his knowledge of water's slant disciplines.
Frost will topple a slapdash cairn

in a season. It takes a humble man to know
gaps matter more in a wall than stone,

making a window on what's really there.
A view, some people. Nothing. Air.

Dinah Livingstone

Maytime

He and she walked out into a May meadow
and made love under a flowering tree.
The sun lit the buttercups
among the new green grass
and shone on the shape of each fresh leaf
pushed out by a rush of juice.
A bird chorus described the sweetness
up to the soft surrounding blue.
The ground was damp and smelt of home.

My beloved is agile and strong
and delicate as a leaping deer.
Come to me. Come.
Then in bliss they rested.

She cupped in her hand
what was now as little and sticky
as a just hatched chick.
Uccellino, he told her and smiled
irresistibly. She kissed him.
After a while: *Eppur si muove -*
it *does* move - he said.

Happy, they laughed
and - honouring great Galileo
who fought for the truth
about what our earth is and does,
against false religion,
and cocked a snook
at the priests in black gowns
on his deathbed -
they made love again.

This

The plane tree is a naked giant now,
its lacy and bobbled
delicate tracery revealed,
sharp against blue. Shape.
Its huge soul winters out.
I absorb its quiet in admiration.

How bodied the pigeon is
when it perches on bare branch.
Yesterday I saw one sat,
as if rehearsing
the twelve days of Christmas,
but in a plum tree.

Its beady amber eye gleamed
on the deep gold fruits,
little magic lanterns still attached,
though all the leaves had gone.
The birdness of that bird:
its being made me glad.

Bird and tree are
and so are we.
Who needs God
when we share such selfhood?

Isn't God merely a codeword
meaning our human kind of self
not only is
but may become
what we imagine
in love and poetry?

The Excluded

Standing on London Bridge on a dreary day
I looked down at the grey river.
I entered the crying.
I heard the keen agony of the lonely,
the roaring of the ignored,
the fury of the defeated,
the tortured screaming an ultimate No,
protest at all the unjust lessening,
weakening as the life force ebbed away.
Wasted. In that chorus, one note
in my own voice told me how it was.

Thousand upon thousand
of the excluded crowded in,
rank on rank of sorrow.
I had not thought there would be so many
uttering that intolerable sound,
beyond the range of the authorities,
who did not have ears to hear it.
But that ultrasonic pitch had greater power
than any laser to shatter the city,
with all its gates and bridges,
however magnificent and strong.

See how it stands desolate
like a hut in a cucumber field,
possession of the hedgehog and pools of tears.
Will that tomorrow ever come
when the crying is comforted,
the weeping wiped away?

Will the dispossessed inherit the earth,
the beautiful pillars of peace be built?
Will eager boys climb trees to watch
and hang like fruit on a clear blue night,
while multitudes stand on London Bridge
exulting in the Easter fireworks,
starbursts flowering for the festival?

Mairi MacInnes

Mass

1

Someone said in a dream, 'Flying's dead easy -
just give yourself to the air.'
It was true: I tripped on a top stair
and took off like a frisbee.
Stairs rivered beneath in the hall's arroyo,
suns flashed through windows,
and I saw that the carpet
approached like a rig of flowered silk
or the leaf canopy of a rain forest -
and I caught at a bough or strut banister
and dropped down unhurt.

Yet unexpectedly the forest
still went past, and how dense,
how weighty and immediate,
the outer world was!
I still floated, I did not exist
minute after minute but in a burst,
all at once, weightless, a rocket
that fired its stars before it fell.

2

Last night there was rain
after a summer of drought
and mushrooms cropped in old pasture.
Today I met women gathering them,
a line seen far-off climbing the hill,
their faces touched by the October sun,
strung out, stooped, companionable,
mothers and the mothers of mothers,
neighbours from the village.
I hailed them as a newcomer
out on my own, and they rose up

full height and gazed, gentle as giraffes,
and immediately from crammed baskets
offered me mushrooms . . . weightless
nothing food, food of the dead.

At its moist uncanny touch I felt
the skin on my fingertips to be
no less than the skin of my life,
so heavy and immediate I was,
so dense and full of earth.

Kathleen McPhilemy

Housewife

Sealed in a bubble of sunlight
a woman is peeling potatoes;
parings coil from her blade
the potatoes are yellow-white, smooth
as her face which holds no darkness.

The house is half-lived in, but yes
she is happy, walled from the darkness:
rooms without plaster, crumbling
floorboards, slime that creeps up
from the cellar, roof-slates
gapped to an unstarred sky.

And the noon-blue wall of her garden
is also a screen against darkness,
yet she smiles, for it's only in dreams
that drag her to waking, she sees
the back of the house is burning
and screams.

Birth of a Child

In that last unreasonable rush of pain
he came: I held him, warm and slippery
with a bright eye and black, unexpected, hair.
I felt so strongly, such unreasoning delight
I can hardly bear to write about
and I have photographs at home
I would not show you, they reveal
a face peeled of all pretence
of all defence.

I always hid my feelings in a drawer
sought to be the second in the room;
so when I write, I equals he or she
I becomes third party, distance comes from order

feelings are made public and disowned.
But only through myself, I understand my friends
why one who shuns the drift flees back to God
and others, who make lesser propitiations,
enrich the analysts.

So who am I to criticize? I hide
inside a silence or in written locked-up words
until I see my twins go down the road
like the children in the Start-Rite poster who
step out assured of earth's continuance.

In the burnt-out forests of the future
animals without eyes stumble and starve.
The skies turn black and at noon
there is the brightness only of moonlight.
In those devastated days there are no
individuals, and hope finally dies.

Mary MacRae

Free Fall

On the edge, scarcely caught
    by gravity's pull,
an astronaut
        or topsy-turvy deep
        sea diver, balanced to keep
giddy ledge-perched feet, hands, eyes steady

in the face of so much
    blue, I pierce air, drop
sight-lines to touch
        rock, shoal, submarine cliff
        close-up, all as clear as if
immaterial. A blotched boulder's

lapped by lazy wave-slaps
    in transparent green
surge and relapse
        and is suddenly thrust
        clean out of the water, just
like a man in a sleek bronze helmet

in lift-off to the sun.
    What kind of merman
is this? Not one
        to trust as he slips on
        a glossy fur pelt, flips on
his back, gazes at me and smiles with

seal-brown, beckoning eyes
    as if expecting
I'd recognise
        and greet him. And it's true,
        some place I know him, in blue
floodlit depths where wave folds over wave

and we slowly rotate,
    selkie skin to skin,
suspended weight -
      less as I smooth his slick
      nape, listen to the rhythmic
long-drawn breaths, my head against his chest.

Sarah Maguire

Communion

I

We both might wonder what you're doing here
till you take refuge from your hunger in my fridge
and then come out with something

that we share the name for: *choriço picante.*
I watch you pierce
the raw meat with a fork

and hold it in the naked ring of gas
until the skin is charred and blistered black
until the stove enamel's measled red.

Slit it down the side
and open out its bleeding heart -
ruddy, vivid, rough.

II

We cannot speak each other's tongue
and so you open up your shirt
to give me signs, to show your wounds.

I know this much:
that, as a child, you fled to Lisbon from Luanda
with a bayonet wound a foot long

(never sutured)
that now grows on your arm
as though a snake's embossed there;

that your skin was punched with shot
which, ten years later, form the dark stigmata
branded on your legs and arms.

III

Take this pungent flesh into your mouth
and staunch your hunger.
Eat.

The Invisible Mender (My First Mother)

I'm sewing on new buttons
to this washed silk shirt.
Mother-of-pearl,
I chose them carefully.
In the haberdashers on Chepstow Place
I turned a boxful over
one by one,
searching for the backs with flaws:
those blemished green or pink or aubergine,
small birthmarks on the creamy shell.

These afternoons are short,
the sunlight buried after three or four,
sap in the cold earth.
The trees are bare.
I'm six days late.
My right breast aches so
when I bend to catch a fallen button
that strays across the floor.
Either way,
there'll be blood on my hands.

Thirty-seven years ago you sat in poor light
and sewed your time away,
then left.
But I'm no good at this:
a peony of blood gathers on my thumb, falls
then widens on the shirt like a tiny, opening mouth.

I think of you like this -
as darkness comes,
as the window that I can't see through
is veiled with mist
which turns to condensation
slipping down tall panes of glass,
a mirror to the rain outside -
and I know that I'll not know
if you still are mending in the failing light,
or if your hands (as small as mine)
lie still now, clasped together, underground.

Barbara Marsh

Wall

I am not hollow.
One tap and I sing like a Tibetan bowl
    soar high as Cassiopeia
    gather harmonics like clouds.
Desert-throated
thick with dirge in my basest of notes
one touch and l am a chorus.

I have become a chain
    linked within the speed of silence
    that reverberates, cone-shaped, through hardness
until I am ringed with hiccups and stutters
    the only sound an 'ah'
    when I open my mouth.
Notes, like thoughts, have trickled out
slithered into drains wet with sludge.

I tiptoe through fragments
in this house of clay
    to find moments of you that are stone:
onyx eggs, I roll them in my hand
    smooth them in the webbing between fingers.
Cool as dawn, I press them against my cheek
    chill the blisters off my skin
where no words have cut through.
Wait for the silence to break.

Gerda Mayer

Male Butterflies Court Falling Leaves

Male butterflies court falling leaves
And male frogs mount galoshes;
Nature exuberantly sways
In dingy mackintoshes;

Or plugs itself into some wild
Or odd sex-aiding symbol,
In desperate hilarity,
In deeply-earnest gambol.

Love has a bash. It needn't end
In flower, fruit or future:
There's profligacy, waste; there is
The seediness of nature.

The Town
Karlsbad/Karlovy Vary

Is it an irony that I return
with a heart so trembling,
I who was ever its stepchild?
It begrudged
shelter to my ancestors.
It spat me out.
It welcomes me now
cautiously
as a guest
who comes
& goes again.
It has changed
its language;
it calls itself
by a new name.
It speaks neither my mother
tongue nor the

language of my enemies
(which is the same);
its voice will be
foreign & strangely
neutral and that too
will be difficult
to endure.
It is an irony that I return
as if hailed, as if hallowed,
like its own true love.
I shall fall at its green feet.

Elma Mitchell

Thoughts After Ruskin

Women reminded him of lilies and roses.
Me they remind rather of blood and soap,
Armed with a warm rag, assaulting noses,
Ears, neck, mouth and all the secret places:

Armed with a sharp knife, cutting up liver,
Holding hearts to bleed under a running tap,
Gutting and stuffing, pickling and preserving,
Scalding, blanching, broiling, pulverising,
- All the terrible chemistry of their kitchens.

Their distant husbands lean across mahogany
And delicately manipulate the market,
While safe at home, the tender and the gentle
Are killing tiny mice, dead snap by the neck,
Asphyxiating flies, evicting spiders,
Scrubbing, scouring aloud, disturbing cupboards,
Committing things to dustbins, twisting, wringing,
Wrists red and knuckles white and fingers puckered,
Pulpy, tepid. Steering screaming cleaners
Around the snags of furniture, they straighten
And haul out sheets from under the incontinent
And heavy old, stoop to importunate young,
Tugging, folding, tucking, zipping, buttoning,
Spooning in food, encouraging excretion,
Mopping up vomit, stabbing cloth with needles,
Contorting wool around their knitting needles,
Creating snug and comfy on their needles.

Their huge hands! their everywhere eyes! their voices
Raised to convey across the hullabaloo,
Their massive thighs and breasts dispensing comfort,
Their bloody passages and hairy crannies,
Their wombs that pocket a man upside down!

And when all's over, off with overalls,

Quickly consulting clocks, they go upstairs,
Sit and sigh a little, brushing hair,
And somehow find, in mirrors, colours, odours,
Their essences of lilies and of roses.

Vulnerable

Everything is vulnerable at sunrise.
Houses are blurred at the edge by the creeping light.
They are not yet upright, not yet property.

Inside the houses
Bodies and beds are still to be disentangled,
Naked, bearded, sheeted, flowing, breathing,
With no cosmetic except the morning's colouring.

No body has had time to put on its uniform
To arm itself with the safe and usual phrases,
To start counting, considering, feeling hungry,
Being man or woman ...

They lie scattered, invisible, soft, lovable,
Under the surreptitious hands of the sunrise,
The touching light.

They are not yet upright, not yet property.

A Clean Sheet

I have wept and slept
And tidied myself up
To stand among the living.

I know daylight will come
Sidling in, grey-faced,
With a ready lie.

I know there is hair in the comb,
A bed to be made.
I know the clock will stroke

The sore with diminishing hands,
And the donkey, work,
Assume its tottering load.

I know proud flesh
Will crawl over the wound
And patch things up

Till nobody would know
Anything had occurred
In the spot where love bled

All night in the teeth of truth
And died hard
To be huddled out of sight

And buried without a word
In an unmarked grave.
                    Now
I smooth a clean sheet

Turn over a new leaf.

Lyn Moir

Auschwitz-Birkenau, December 27th, 1992

Now that you mention it, I cannot say for certain
no birds sing. The air was cold, too cold for song,
for breath. There was a deadened silence, hanging
heavy in the air, cut by sporadic footsteps
on the snow. From time to time a voice escaped
the noose of whispers, drifted uncertainly, and fell.

I can say it was snowing. Not the snow of cards
or Christmas trees, steel needles piercing flesh.
Frost flowers spread, thin-bladed, over window-glass,
filling the frames with unaccustomed privacy.
Outside again, each in our ice-bound world, we moved
apart, grasping at solitude to separate
us from the weight of those accumulated cries.

It is, there's no denying it, a place of death,
fenced in by icicles of madness and of pain,
so cold that day that ice had blocked the jets
of the eternal flame. I shall remember silence,
and wind that slipped inside the skin, and black
and white, stark verticals forever etched
upon the frozen surface of my eyes.

Introduction

I'd thought there would be bells
or fireworks, light, you know
the sort of thing, electric
current zigzagging the place.
I would have settled
for the comforting sensation
of a soft, creased leather glove.

You, just one hand shaken
amongst a dozen in the room,
were not what I expected.

No sparks, no noise;
only my skin: it liquefied
as in an acid bath and, bleached,
my bones reclothed themselves
in your warm flesh and were
no longer mine, while yours contrived
to infiltrate my hollow limbs,
left vacant by defection.

A fair exchange, a physical reaction,
or chemical, depending on your point
of view, something at any rate
which could not be reversed.

Felicity Napier

Jasmine

The hottest July on record - as hot as Spain.
Number fifty-four is a settlement of grief,
shuttered and blind to the street outside.
To a background of the Albinoni that he loved
the telephone rings and rings again, and sounds
of sobbing ebb and flow in the cool, dim rooms.
Jasmine twists around the door, scattering
the step with small white stars. A serpent
hose lies curled asleep on the cracked earth.

Beyond the fence another house is in distress;
its back has been removed. Workmen's radios drone
across the lawn where empty deckchairs listen.
Somewhere a piano is being tuned. Inside,
the dog sprawls, refusing to move; goldfish gobble
for oxygen and the lovebird's cage is silted up.
And visitors visit... some wanted, some not.
She drifts through the rooms, in his new blue shirt
with the chain he gave her glinting at her throat.

Meals around the table they brought back from France
last year are rituals that hold the days together.
Friends bring pizza, pasta, coke for the children
and the first small seedless grapes. In the hall
the stacks of unread newspapers mount; cards and letters
layer the table. And flowers keep coming - drooping
garden roses, glossy pot plants, stiff bouquets.
She has pinned his smiling photograph everywhere -
that lean face, an icon now, continues to shock.

The crisis dwindles. Her friends start to fall away;
the children return to school; the airless nights pass
and yet, like the sickly sweetness of the jasmine,
his absence won't go away. It shadows her all day.
But soon she will learn the art of self-defence:
she won't buy coffee beans or make his lentil soup;
she won't run down a street, pursuing his look-alike.
And, in the dark, sleepless hours, when that clear voice
calls out to her, she'll train her heart not to leap.

Caroline Natzler

To the Scientist Who Showed Me

complexity
a regular beat the sign of a diseased heart
but so alive the crazy heart's awakened leap

how birds are aerodynamically unstable
attentive to air
each flutter an uncertain
communion, which may become a journey

how proteins fold close
touching as many surfaces as possible
in a warm interplay of hints and cues
our livelong process

how life may have evolved in the deep heave
of oceans unsounded by sunlight
in extremity
deliciousness squeezing into being
in the dark flow

and you
my becoming world
(o my universe!)
come belling through my new flushed life
this astonished emptiness

come resounding through
and all is flow

Dorothy Nimmo

Black Parrot

Kill the black parrot. Choke the sodding bird,
it never said a kind thing or a true word
or if it did that wasn't what I heard.

I only heard it squawking in my ear
things no-one in their right mind wants to hear
that made me cold with shame and white with fear.

Behave yourself. Control yourself. You know
you don't think that, you only think you do.
You can't just please yourself. I told you so.

You're being selfish. It's for your own good.
You must. You must not. But you know you should.
If you tried harder I am sure you could.

I'm disappointed in you. Never say
I didn't tell you. But you had your way,
you'd not be told. There'll be a price to pay.

Where was it Polly learned that canting word?
It's time to wring its neck, the stupid bird.

What made us think that was the voice of God?

A Warning

If when you have washed your hands you wash them again
though they are already perfectly clean,
if when you've checked you've got everything -
directions, cash, vaporizer, ticket - you go through
everything again just once more,

if when you are halfway down the street
you think you may not have locked the door
so you go back and yes, it is locked, but you wonder if

you remembered to switch the cooker off
so you go back to make sure,

I have to tell you it's likely to get worse.
Soon you won't be able to leave the house.
You will cram your bag with everything
you possess, you will hide it somewhere
absolutely safe.

You won't know where to put yourself.
You won't know what to do with your hands
so you'll steep them in pure bleach
but they are still offensive
so you pick up a knife.

You have lost your tongue. You have lost
your head. The cooker turns itself on
automatically, the burners are red-hot,
the warning light flashes
the sirens go off.

For Susan and Her Mother

My mother's breasts were little purses
nipple-buttoned. Her voice
rang round the house and all the good glasses
up on the top shelf shivered.

I tugged at her skirt. She was about
her Father's business.

When I had daughters I said
I would mind my own business
but as they grew up I watched them
watching me behind closed faces.

Now is the time for our mothers to fall
like sparrows, their feathers numbered.

You carry yours cupped in your hands
to the hilltop and let her go
winging out above the meadows.
What larks, what sadness
what a cold pink sunset.

And down here I pick out bits of glass.
I splash the window-frames with blood,
the doors, the lintels

and those who are wise go past
minding their own business.

Ruth Padel

Bed-Time

Time to go to bed again. Time for the moon
To get in among the muddle of arms and legs,
     Get completely unstrung and set free
     And hold on to you. Because you've done
All this but are also the one thing
That'll hold me, lost in this narrow room

As if it's Pharaoh's mine of slippery agate,
     Flashing quartz chambers
Where I could wander for years

Now changed to an arch of green cedars
And a wild-honey garden of mist and secret walks
     With cyclamen in the shade, a tiltyard
     Of tiered lawns rising and rising - to sundials, mazes
And driftwood igloos seeing off dew from their walls
At dawn. Because of you. Because of you.

White Horse

Think iridescent. After all the myth stuff
     Of meeting, of coming alive,
We both hit the road. The journey back unfolds
What the down train never showed -

That Tintagel-look-alike castle,
     Not there, I swear, first time round.
To our right, a new-minted sea
Flashes its Book of Hours cerulean

Over British Rail Chicken Tikka Massala,
     Surprising the triple-glazing
With its hug of open gold. The Darley Arabian
In person, sire of racing legend, the original

Snow-thoroughbred, is looking our way
     As if Lancelot caught his steed on polaroid
Before he mounted him,
Then pasted the enlargement on a hill.

Those Druids (think of the mistletoe) - someone
     Had railways and lovers in mind
When they chalked out this boy's stamping-ground.
He's a master of desire, giving the high sign

To our remit into the waking world
     Made newleaf-green as Malory, or the lyre of Iggy Pop.
Also to you beside me, sleepy, almost already
A part of me, turning my skin to fire.

Evangeline Paterson

Knitting Woman

In her chosen corner she sits. Rivers of knitting
cascade plaining and purling over her lap,
winter and summer together. She has her reasons,
knows that sudden contrary August weather
is worse than blizzards in winter, trusts no seasons.

Her young have escaped. She sees them
at large in the world's cold winds. Her anxious care
follows them all by post, in cumbersome parcels,
cabled and striped and ribbed. She knows no ill
that can't be cured in an Aran jacket, or better
endured in a mohair sweater. God
may temper the wind or not, but never
a lamb of hers will ever be caught shorn.

She sits defying hap and circumstance,
weak chests, ill luck, chaos and old night.

She would like to knit the whole world a pullover.

History Teacher in the Warsaw Ghetto Rising

after an engraving by Maurice Mendjisky

The schoolmaster once known as
Umbrella Feet
unfolds his six-foot length
of gangling bone

and, mild as usual,
blinks - his bi-focals
having gone the way of his pipe
and his tree-shaded study
and his wife Charlotte -

and, jacket flapping, as usual,
carpet slippers treading
rubble of smashed cellars,

advancing steadily into the
glare of the burning street

and holding his rifle uncertainly
as if he thought it irrelevant
- as indeed it is -

he leads his scattered handful
of scarecrow twelve-year-olds

towards the last few minutes
of their own brief history.

Meg Peacocke

Visitation

About the dead of August or September.
Motes settling in the airless room,
hearth still in acrid blossom
of pleated paper.
A nap of sunlight, smoothing in
through curtains, touches her, my childless aunt,
brushes her grey skin.
She lifts her arm, suppliant,

waits for the insolent rush of the god
who comes in guise of a macaw,
violently blue and yellow,
rolling the knob of his tongue like a quid
of tobacco. Grasps her. Leans to extract
the striped seed she offers in her lips.
Touching the place his antique foot has marked
she sits back laughing, flushed with worship.

And who's a good boy then? He's come
heavily home, the ginger man,
chained stomach, oiled hair,
theatrical at the door. *How's Mac?*
(Now now, be good!) And how's my girl?
watching her smile. The bird
shuts one licorice eye. She takes the ritual kiss,
unlocks the tantalus, pours whisky.

Broody

Lifted, she's a sleeper
jostled in the dead time:
puffed, claggy-feathered.

Begins, step and step.
Close, open, stretch.
An old dancer limbering up.

Nibbles a dish of rain.
At each sip raises
her obsidian beak, like praying.

Shudders, curvets
on cramped lizard legs
and flaps, and shrieks. Subsides.

Taps at a grain or two.
Clucks sotto voce. (Was that the way
the tune went?) Stertorously, shits.

Lifted back, she settles
to the twelve eggs like a coracle
gaining still water;
shuffles down, and broods.

Three Reflections on the Creation of Man

Michelangelo: panel in the Sistine Chapel

In the beginning, Adam, warm as new milk,
drowsing on the pomegranate crust of the world
his eyes filled with the colour of distance
        and already there will be primroses in the combe of his back
        a weasel questing for eggs
        a blackbird after berries
        an adder coiled in the eye of the sun.

In the beginning, the Ancient of Days
robed in a whirling conch of departure
with flamen and hierophant and the cry of cherubim
        and already he has caused the pallid sky
        to flood between his finger and Adam's; separation
        echoes interminably from hand to hand.

In the beginning, under God's rooted arm
Eve like a foxcub, quick for danger and delight.
She has tasted the blood of loss and making
        and already she trusts no one
        gives nobody her hand
        knowing that stories contradict
        and apples will not keep.

Pascale Petit

Embrace of the Electric Eel

For thirty-five years, Father, you were a numb-fish,
I couldn't quite remember what it felt like

that last time you hugged me when I was eight,
just before you went away.

But when you summon me to your stagnant pool,
Dad, Papa, whatever I should call the creature

that you are, now you finally ask for my love:
do you think I've become strong as the horses

Humboldt forced into a stream
to test the voltage of Amazonian eels?

He had never witnessed
"such a picturesque spectacle of nature"

as those great eels clamped against the bellies
of his threshing horses, how their eyes

almost popped out and their manes stood on end.
Though the jolt alone did not kill them,

many were so stunned they drowned.
That's how it is, Father, when you open your arms

and press your entire length against my trunk.

Mirador

When Gran fell downstairs and died I wanted to visit her house,
stand on top of the stairs and at the bottom
and on each step between her life and death.
I climbed carefully as once I'd climbed through cloud forest
over the tangle of roots on my way to see

Angel Falls from the mirador of Alexander Laime.

When I reached the lookout point where the whole cataract
can be viewed, sweat in my eyes and needle-fine spray,
there was drizzle, a driving wind,
dark clouds obscured the head of the falls.
For about a third of a mile up the amphitheatre
I saw how water after it has fallen so far
seems to flow back up then fall again
as air - spirals, comets, flames.

I thought of Jimmy Angel, discoverer of these falls,
how, after his death, his wife Marie
had a bush pilot fly her right up to the head
where sudden cloud can cause a crash.
And against the winds she opened the cockpit window
to throw his ashes, spray burning her face.
Then Laime the hermit built his hut on Rat Island
so he could watch dawn turn the plummeting waters to fire.

All night Gran was restless as rockets exploded
and fireworks lit up her uncurtained windows.
By four a.m. the ninety years of her life gathered forces
against the torrent that battered the panes.
Nine hundred metres to fall from the summit.
Bone and water, bone and air, the corridors
in sandstone where marrow has carved passages,
the base so strewn with rocks I could not see the plunge-pool.

But when I went and stood in Gran's hall, looking up
at the air that contained aftershocks and echoes,
the air I wanted to collect in boxes and label,
as I'd scooped the red soil at the foot of the falls
for proof of my visit, it was as if I was underwater,
all my childhood in her house falling on my head,
against my eyes, down my mouth, all the water and fire of my life.

What She Wanted

What she wanted was to return
to the original rainforest

hear water pushing
through the sapwood

and leaves eating light
as she wanted to eat light.

She knew her nature
was to be water, not wood.

She knew there was a grove
of vertical rivers

of roaring waterfall-trees,
and a grove of whirlpool-trees

with vortices she could dive through,
past the hollow years of her life

right back to the roots.

Patricia Pogson

Amaryllis Belladonna

I cannot like you -
this sudden switch
from male to female;
that shrivelled foreskin
sloughed to reveal splayed buds.

Oscar would have sprayed
attar of roses on
your immaculate skirt,
changed the decor to match
your waxy extravagance.

Beardsley would have drawn
your attenuated stalk:
thin phallus whose wicked point
blossoms pink lillies
to sacrifice by candlelight ...

and David Bowie would become you
(the perfect deviant):
odourless, epicene,
tinted exotic
on a hollow stick.

You

You were my salt, my starch, the rock
under my feet, my bit of rough,
the gradient that made my muscles tough
- I'll need them now to get me out of hock.

I play your old-style movers, shakers
non-stop till the stylus wearies.
The neighbours must be tiring of Chet Baker's
melancholy trumpet, Blossom Dearie's
girlish intrigues, Fats Waller's double bluff.

I wear your sweaters. Kept your coat.
I've got your last tape, stumbling, gruff,
dozen of snaps of you, us, the first note
you sent me, practical, no soppy stuff.
Just marks on paper. Not enough.

The Coil

You can't not live with ghosts
their knock and jostle.

Habits that wear you.
That thing with the kettle flex.
Taps so tight they hurt your wrist.
Making fifth gear a fetish.

Phrases. *Kiss, kiss*, last thing before sleep
his fingers tucked under your hip.
Bollocks snarled at the six o'clock news.

Road signs. *Tiredness can kill.*
Fungi spreading a cool glow at first light.

Places. Gurnal Dubs. Brow Foot.
The gate near the twisted larch.
Counting shooting stars on the Crook road.
Last stretch of motorway,
Farleton Knott pointing the way home.

Better get close. Only a short spit
before they make you their own.

Peggy Poole

Not the berry, not the dark

for A.P.

Some tell of the wood's music,
wood used to fashion bellows;
others speak of the berry
that is the heart of the wine,
dark bunches gathered in autumn
to mellow winter evenings.

I sing not of the berry
nor the bark, but of white florets
that contain within them
long sought powers of healing.

Others may speak of the darkness
the black world of the blind
but you, who have never seen
the youngest of your children,
tell of years in perpetual sunlight
of needing the balm of night
and how elder blossom brought
a measure of merciful dimness,
while to some it has given sight.

I speak of the white witch
who, after collecting clusters
to accomplish her good spells,
says with reverence to the tree:
"Madam, I thank thee."

Joan Poulson

The King Was In -

That meal last night too rich, too much
and later
our bedroom chokingly hot.

She lay beside me
breath light as moths wing
eyelids (indigo-fringed) fluttering on her cheeks
pillow-soft body resistant as flint
her sleep unbroken.

Now she paces the corridors
new robe hissing round her ankles
fingers lingering over stitchery, hips prominence
curve of thigh

caressing silken bees: padded, plump
on mulberry taffeta.

I smell her skin, sugared cinnamon
through my locked door
feel its sheen against my palm

curve my thumb around
this guinea's perfection, lay it
lip overlapping lip on this glistening mound...
but must lie down, rest. My chest iron-bound
by her

entering her parlour
leaving the door open so I hear her
humming her songs
creamy throat vibrating
coiled red-gold braids framing the waxed oval of her face.

Clink of spoon on pot
scooping up mounds of pollened sweetness
seeking
fragments of comb.

Soon she will replace the lid
return, rattle the handle of my door.

I shall ignore her
but she will persist.

Then . . . I shall call out
inform her I am counting.
Perhaps give a little yawn.

Caroline Price

House Hunting

The hallway coughs its stale breath
into our faces. Dust shifts
in the grates. Between net and pane,
the splayed brilliance
of a small tortoiseshell, propped
like a scrap of painted card,

trapped behind glass
like the bridal pair, the child
ankle-deep in sand,
the old man in a garden chair
clasping a cat, head tilted to one side
as if he can hear from there

the silence of the sewing machine
in an upstairs room
where a fusty skirt is caught mid-repair,
the needle hanging,
treadle poised
for the foot to descend again;

sitting there still as the sun still warms
the garden, the derelict frames,
stirring the plants inside
into further life: they press themselves
against the glass, bent double
straining for cracks,

for the lids to be lifted, for us
to release them, unravel their limbs;
to finish the seam and bite the thread,
call in the child,
open a window
and let the butterfly go.

Green Fingers

He plunges into the garden like a man
who wants to drown,
plants out Red Robins by the score,
fingers ramming into the earth, his nails
black rinds, all over his skin
the sweet rubbed smell of tomato sap
disguising everything.

She trims the edges of the endless lawn
as if each blade
must be the same, the *snip snip*
filling her eyes, stains on her jeans
spreading where she kneels
stubbornly, inch by inch
grinding the grass down.

Evening after evening. Dusk falls,
a moon does
or doesn't show. Sometimes it rains.
They press on into the darkness,
their ungloved hands moving
whitely, blindly
as fish spawned underground.

They do not say a word to each other.
They talk non-stop
to the seedlings, urge on the shrubs
and are still amazed that everything riots
around them, while at their backs
self-seeded honesty
rattles thin rounds like applause.

Azincourt

Under this *drap de blanc* there could be
anything. Snow levels the land
to a frozen canvas you proceed
to write on - names, the date -
with a dark-tipped branch snapped from
an early blackthorn,

already putting this moment
in the past, this disputed ground
where we stood in February
shoulder to shoulder, unfurling
our own quick breath, on edge
for any sound

and saw how words would fill
and fade away, hoofprints, footprints
vanish beneath light or grass
or water or a thousand
other feet; how everything that happened
would be erased,

leaving at most a remnant, a small
souvenir: so others coming here
would stare around like us
and see the stick jammed
in the earth, landed where you
had loosed it, tilted, quivering.

Kathleen Raine

Her Room

At first, not breathed on,
Not a leaf or a flower knew you were gone,
Then, one by one,

The little things put away,
The glass tray
Of medicines empty,

The poems still loved
Long after sight failed
With other closed books shelved,

And from your cabinet
Remembrances to one and another friend
Who will forget

How the little owl, the rose-bowl,
The Brig-o'Doone paperweight,
The Japanese tea-set

Lived on their shelf, just here,
So long, and there,
Binding memories together,

Binding your love,
Husband and daughter in an old photograph,
Your woven texture of life

A torn cobweb dusted down,
Swept from the silent room
That was home.

Your Gift of Life Was Idleness

Your gift of life was idleness,
As you would set day's task aside
To marvel at an opening bud,
Quivering leaf, or spider's veil
On dewy grass in morning spread.
These were your wandering thoughts, that strayed
Across the ever-changing mind
Of airy sky and travelling cloud,
The harebell and the heather hill,
World without end, where you could lose
Memory, identity and name
And all that you beheld, became,
Insect wing and net of stars
Or silver-glistering wind-borne seed
For ever drifting free from time.
What has unbounded life to do
With body's grave and body's womb,
Span of life and little room?

Irene Rawnsley

On Wether Fell

This is where she scattered his ashes like seed
and some was pecked by birds
who occupy the air above lake and valley,

and some leached underground
to become the restless voice of rain
searching the hollow hill,
the wind's messages drummed on a stormy day
down Wensleydale into Hawes.

Now he's the stuff of yellow tormentil,
a path of stars in the tough grass,
creeping thistle, eyebright, thyme,
the torn web of a spider,
moss on a stone, moon mushrooms.

Bird, wind, water, cloud, seed, season,
he has been written into the script.
The hill's long afterwards won't rub him out.

Michèle Roberts

mayday mayday

The fields here tick over
with dandelion clocks
fragile and full
as luminous as moons.

Your room smells of fish and shit.
You curl in your nightie
a clack of bones.
Your guts are plastic
gartered to your thin thigh.

Down the lane the maypole
shakes out its ribbons
on pointed toes.
Solemn and quick
the children's knees skip up.
Sandals and anoraks.
Print frocks as
sharp as lettuces. Your
death dances forwards. Your
death dances back.

I do what I can:
bleed the fridge dry
hack up the chicken for soup
rip milky weeds from the grass.

You thrash on.
Death's hooks in
your belly, your mouth.

You're so pale. Parched
as these London streets
cracking up in the heat.

The butcher's in Holloway Road
gusts forth the smell of warm blood.

Your voice on the telephone
stumbles: so far away.

I slept in your attic
looking over the long hill.
The open window let in
cold sweet darkness
impersonal stars
sheep crying in the night.

Anne Ryland

Silk Escape Map

I hold the land of Burma in my hands
as if it were a live creature
breathing into me,
sent to preserve us both until the end.

After my years of wear and tear
and the plainness of wartime material,
escape glows dimly through this map.
I search for you once more
in the clarity of its print.

At night I prowl the ripples of enemy lines,
silent map smuggled inside a bamboo cane.
With blistered fingers I shoot at snakes
and peel off leeches.
The jungle rustles.

In the early hours I sample names
on my parched tongue,
Yenangyaung. Taungdwingyi . . .
drawing closer to that place where you are.

White days pass by as I allow myself
to flow again, to eat without the guilt
of your grey rice ration.
I spin our cocoon within me.

Your few written words were rotting
before they even reached me;
your spoken words I have concealed
in a small hollow,
unsoiled by temperature.

If you are set free, and return,
I am afraid now
that the pattern of me will startle you.
Oceans stream down my arms,
I am the coolness and lustre of silk.

Below the red eye of a sun
which probes you slowly each day,
you are a tiny flightless creature,
prisoner of heat and dust.
But the single filament of you, unreeled,
is thousands of miles long.

Julie Sampson

1894: Fran Skating on the Manor Pond

She skates over and around its frozen surface,
then spins a pencil-pirouette,
muffs blue-heat her hands
and from her waist a scarlet whirl of skirt.
In hazy light veins seem to break in olive eyes
as the blades of her boots refract the scratching ice
and under setting sun
her shadow is half a pulsating heart.

Ida, in the kitchen sits and snips
the corners of the paper folds.
Brittle like ice.
Deft, her fingers snip and snap then
rippling like a fan the row of skating dolls
holding hand by hand.

Robert, in the other room,
turns a page.
His book about the Ministry
is a weight upon his mind.

His sisters are making their mark;
each enacts a secret lore
on a slated sheet of white,
figure skating on the land of open-space
and inscribing a serrated pictograph.

Even the tiny feet of each minute dancing doll
are chipped away to equip them with the sharpest razor cut.

Ann Sansom

Delta

Open your eyes.
A parched bandage is uncoiling on your arm.
You feel no pain, no fear: your brain
has been drawn out with hooks, preserved in alcohol.
You are merely the kernel of a wooden shell,
but I am here, in the gloom, the frail rushlight,
the suggestion of spears, chariot wheels,
the small longboat at your feet.
Bronze mirrors lean like a corridor.
Don't be deceived. This is a sealed room.

Lie down and wait.
Comfort yourself with dreams.
Sand will go on sifting itself into a recessed door
but, in time, a dome raised cubits high
will open on familiar sky. Yes. It will.
A caravan will pass, returning home.
Believe yourself in it, a traveller, moving
among those who sell food at the roadside,
among the gaudy stalls of beads, rugs, nets...

Listen.
There is music, water on the floodtide,
ibis and white geese rising
rowdy as Cleethorpes gulls. Hold this thought
and you have Calor gas seeping sweet as mildew
in a tomb; an umbrella, pushchair, skateboard
propped against a brown formica partition.

Lie down and wait.
Consider your knees. A pyramid in the sheet.
Your arm. No longer embalmed but burned
last night when you were frying fish,
too pissed to read the zigzag hieroglyphs
of a car-battery telly...
Pursue this fantasy. It may release you.

Carole Satyamurti

from: **Between the Lines**

I

Words were dust-sheets, blinds.
People dying randomly, for 'want of breath',
shadowed my bed-times.
Babies happened;
adults buried questions under bushes.

Nouns would have been too robust
for body-parts; they were
curt, homeless prepositions - 'inside',
'down there', 'behind', 'below'. No word
for what went on in darkness, overheard.

Underground, straining for language
that would let me out, I pressed to the radio,
read forbidden books. And once
visited Mr Cole. His seventeen
budgerigars praised God continually.

He loved all words, he said, though he used
few to force a kiss. All that summer
I longed to ask my mother, starved myself,
prayed, imagined skirts were getting tight,
hoped jumping down ten stairs would put it right.

My parents fought in other rooms,
their tight-lipped murmuring muffled
by flock wallpaper.
What was wrong, what they had to say
couldn't be shared with me.

He crossed the threshold in a wordless
slam of doors. 'Gone to live near work'
my mother said, before she tracked down
my diary, broke the lock, made me cut out
pages that guessed what silence was about.

Intensive Care

Your voice silenced by tubes,
the mute, continual cough lifts you awake.
I stroke your hair; you stare at me,
eyes remote, tearless.

You write, 'I'm hungry.'
I watch each breath
sucked in between your ribs,
beg for you.

You lie as if in state
too dignified.
If I thought you were leaving me
from this white room

with only plastic pillows for your journey
I would cram your hands with anemones,
snatch out the canula, enfold you,
run with you to where the band is playing.

But now, as my hands
make shadow creatures on the wall,
I read your lips: 'rhinoceros',
know I have you still.

Ourstory

Let us now praise women
with feet glass slippers wouldn't fit;

not the patient, nor even the embittered
ones who kept their place,

but awkward women, tenacious with truth,
whose elbows disposed of the impossible;

who split seams, who wouldn't wait,
take no, take sedatives;

who sang their own numbers, went uninsured,
knew best what they were missing.

Our misfit foremothers are joining forces
underground, their dusts mingling

breast-bone with scapula, forehead
with forehead. Their steady mass

bursts locks; lends a springing foot
to our vaulting into enormous rooms.

Woman Bathing in a Stream:

Rembrandt

Just 'woman'.
We know it was your Hendrickje,
who bore your daughter,
reared your son,
fed you, clothed and sheltered you,
sat, stood, lay down for you,
and who, even in death,
kept you from creditors.
Almost everything we know of her
is what she did for you.

I'm angry for her
- that you took everything,
made her a vehicle for light,
shadow and reflection
and gave her only anonymity
- as now, in fashion photographs:
dress by Cardin,
hat by David Shilling,
ear-rings, necklace by Adrian Mann
and a model with no name.

Yet I can see how you refused to prettify
the ungainly shift, hoisted to hip level,
thick thighs, peasant forearms, shoulders;
how you seem to have felt their balance,
understood her spirit weight
- painted almost in her idiom.
She must have known - no wonder, then,
the serene half-smile, lack of artifice.
Being so recognized
perhaps made simple fame irrelevant.

Myra Schneider

A Letter to Sujata in Bremen

You've been here, seen the frilled curtains,
the diamond panes in Morton Way,
and all the trees restrained on verges.
But I must imagine Mozartstrasse,
the house where you live, your landlady.
Is there a girl on the floor above yours
who sits at a piano playing tunes
from 'The Wonder Boy', a book I was given
when I was eight? I can hear
'Eine Kleine Nachtmusik' - its notes,
clustered droplets of light sparkling
on the ceilings and walls of tall rooms.

And suddenly - you'll smile at this -
my mouth is watering, my head's crammed
like a shop window in Salzburg,
with boxes of Mozartkugeln, each
gold-papered and stamped with a picture
of the genius fastened in tight lace,
in a jacket red as haws.

Do you know these chocolate globes?
Of course they have nothing to do
with the giddy living, the intensity,
the rush of patterned sounds to the brain;
nothing to do with the envy, the complaints
about too many notes, the fluctuating success.
Or Mozart dying, maybe poisoned
by his medicine, with poverty at the door.

So I knew my sketches
of 18 Mozartstrasse were only fantasies
even before I read your story
about the damenschneider who lived
and worked at your address before the war,
who sent his Jewish wife to America,

who disappeared along with his scissors,
cottons, sewing machine. Nothing remained
but pins and needles littering the floors.
Those days so many thinned into air,
leaving neither wisp nor whisper.

As my childhood ended - years before
you were born - scraps began to surface
about the cruelty to Jews in the War.
I stuffed the horror under the carpet,
buried guilt inside myself,
trembled that I was a Jew.

And even now, Sujata, I turn off
documentaries about concentration camps,
afraid terror will march through my sleep
and wakefulness for the rest of my life.
Yet there are sentences I've read
that are red-hot needles embedded in me:
'Every person had one small bowl
to eat from, drink from, piss in.
We washed ourselves in our urine.'
'Mothers were made to watch . . .'

I try to imagine someone
who's tortured women and children,
going home, kissing his daughter,
moved to tears by a piano concerto.
I fail . . .

But here is a fragment that's survived
all the years since 1941:
Frau Schneider, my husband's grandmother,
stick thin, widowed, eighty,
was dragged from her flat in Vienna.
Wedged between the jeering neighbours
was the daughter who'd been astute enough
to bury her identity and resurrect herself
with blonde hair and Christian names.
Mouth full of helplessness, she watched
her screaming mother borne away...

This sub-zero December morning
I take an envelope out of a drawer,
write your address: 18 Mozartstrasse,
think of Cherubino's questioning song,
its notes that flutter and stab ecstasy;
the bittersweet weavings of violins,
how the clarinet soars trilling light.
Then I shiver and touch my pale flesh
- how many lost tailors, how many
last sightings of grandmothers?

The Red Cupboard

after a painting by Bonnard

is wide open. It is not rage
        that's ripening
in this recess. In the swell of heat
no bonfire flames are ripping
into wood. Linings and shelves
radiate cardinal, damson,
        coronation reds,
the utterness I long for daily.

The cool of vases, upturned glasses
        with quiet stems,
a plate propped on its rim affirm
the everyday. The small globes
could be transparent eggs,
egg-shaped apples. But the apples
        are weighty
as earthenware, shine like china.

Why am I feeding this passion
        for seeing
one thing as another: reflections
that throw light, intensify, extend
yet meddle with the original? I want
untouched, the apple-sweetness
        that sifts
through racks, lofts, hall passages.

Impossible. Every apple
　　I touch
is the alphabet's start, a wrinkled mouth,
the curve of a cheek that persists
from dream. And these on the shelf
are a tempting red, from the garden
　　where Eve
picked, from all my gardens.

So where does it lead, this opening?
　　To the night
under the stairs with cocoa, blankets,
no roughnesses in mother,
to the longing at my core, a wanting
that can never be satisfied
　　Yet inside
the red cupboard nothing is denied.

Leave Taking

And when he was struck speechless
then I wanted him to speak again,
when he couldn't deliver the orders
I wanted to cram back into his mouth,
break the unbearable waters
of wrath over my head
then I wanted to hear his voice again,
would have held out cupped hands
for a command, a judgement, a complaint.

When he was sentenced
to a wordless struggle for breath
and could no longer devour us
with: 'I'm dying...I wish I was dead,'
I discovered what I'd guessed:
he'd cried wolf instead of pain,
stalked by implacable terrors
he dared not name. But he'd given
doctors instructions to haul him
back for the last mile, last inch

to keep tabs on the world,
its disgraceful conduct of itself,
his daughters' failings, successes
and the complex finances in his head.
Minutes before his lungs
finally rebelled
his fingers plotted in the air
the upward curve of a grandson's career.

And in those four speechless days
when his eyes fixed
on the precise saline drip
drip through glass arteries,
when his hands washed themselves
of the universe or clutching at a pen
produced strange new writing,
did a kind of acceptance trickle through?

In those four days
I began to strip him of shortcomings,
bury the terrible damages
and I hung onto his zest,
his generosities, his ever-
enquiring scientific mind,
his hunger for consciousness,
that miracle each person carries,
a delicate globe lit
by intricate, unseen filaments
which is so suddenly put out,
which is totally
irreplaceable.

Flood

Last night rain begged, badgered
to enter my room, share my sheets.
I heard it ramming itself into the hole
in the guttering, felt it sink the garden,
drown pale hundreds of spread
sycamore hands and I knew the stream
in the park had swollen to a busy tongue
greedy for grass. In the dark of my head

flowered that first environmentalist,
Noah, who rated the world's species
highly as family. I saw him cooped
with milk-heavy cows, the mustard heat
of lion, pestered by droves of fearful voices.
Butterflies speckled the wooden dimness
with yellow, bee humming rose from the ark's belly.

When blue squeezed between the clouds
the old man climbed to the third storey
where owl moons and pigeon beads
lit a windowless attic. He lifted down
a dove and, mobbed by anxious relatives,
sent it into a cauldron of light. At last
he lay on the new green world's solid body
under a stretched cloth of rainbow.

But rain still pecked at my panes
and at sleep's border I found myself in the ark
designed by today's saviour - a sealed capsule
sleek as a whale that stabled two
of every make of car and carried a notice:
No animals for hygenic reasons.
The immense plastic bubble rode on waters
that stilled the North Circular Road,
its goose-grey flyovers, flucrescent cities.

I awoke to sunlight, to seagulls swimming
on a rippling glitter in the park's basin,
willow limbs splayed on a path.
And though squirrels whisked down
damp trunks to claw at the pale gold
of leaves, though children waded in pools
alive with bright pieces of sky,

I couldn't wipe the end of my vision:
how nothing remained after the ebbing
but tree stubs, concrete posts,
a few wheel hubs, mute screens,
mobile phones stuck in a limbo of mud,
how the world shrank to an over-used
tennis ball in the palm of my hand.

Ruth Sharman

The Travancore Evening Brown

As if by naming it I were naming you,
who've learnt to mimic withered leaves
and fade into the shadows; as if a name
could pin down all that's fragile
and sounds could recreate the patterns
of who you are and what you know,

I'm raiding your store, eager to know
why this name means so much to you,
learning about his violet patterns
and underwings like withered leaves,
her browns a reflection too fragile
for the evening of her name.

That day you mentioned the name
in passing, wanting me to know
how they dance at dusk, as fragile
as shadows, it could have been you
who was dancing, like the bracken leaves
in the wind making silver patterns,

and so I'm weaving patterns
with these thoughts about a name,
building a bridge of shadows and leaves,
making links all too fragile,
since there's no other way I know
to reach out and touch what touches you.

It's this butterfly that touches you,
and those weaving courtship patterns
few of us will ever know,
since the place that shares its name
shelters an existence as fragile
as the memory of light on leaves;

so before it vanishes like leaves,
and names no longer mean as much to you,
I'm gathering in memories as fragile
as leaf shadows or the invisible patterns
of larksong, repeating a name
that dances to a tune only you can know

as if through leaves and shadow patterns
and things as fragile as a name
I could know for certain how to reach you.

Penelope Shuttle

My Son

My son is one of those stars
painted on the silk star chart
made in Dunhuang in 940 AD,

he is one of the doves hidden
but ragged in the three-storeyed
dove-cote along the lane,

he is also a racing pigeon
circling with many others
when my furthest neighbour

casts and twirls his lasso of birds
heavenward,
tugging the sky into a treble noose of noise,

unison that puzzled me so much
buzzing over the garden
like an invisible top, till I understood

his pigeons wore ankle whistles
to make the sky sing,
and when he calls them down -

'come back, come back', into the loft
they obey
in reluctant sky-loving batches,

the last one is my son;

sometimes though
he is an eskimo curlew,
Numenius borealis, almost extinct,

flying over the Hold-with-Hope
Peninsula -
in his bird's eye view

has all the luminous tradition
of the Arctic,
leaping ice, water and light,

mirages, refractions,
wing shadow on ice,
silk star on silk sky,

for he is of that upper element,
he is far yet near,
never yet forever

descending from his flight,
his weight barely grazing me,
alighting in my arms

then relaunching,
will not be called back
from his wherever

among all the others unborn,
winging from me again,
his name is as silk spun from my tongue.

Indoors

House of invisible waterfalls
indoor echoes,

the central heating
whistling through its teeth,

the born blind silences
of the window,

his themes of juniper
and fallen leaf,

a meanwhile of the self
coolly true and untrue,

a felicity of heartbreak,
the falls

chilling and scenting
the house

with brilliant musks
of the unseen,

the sanity
of their no-worse-for-wear floods.

Jungian Cows

In Switzerland, the people call their cows
Venus, Eve, Salome, or Fraulein Alberta,
beautiful names
to yodel across the pastures at Bollingen.

If the woman is busy with child or book,
the farmer wears his wife's skirt
to milk the most sensitive cows.

When the electric milking-machine arrives,
the stalled cows rebel and sulk
for the woman's impatient skilful fingers
on their blowzy tough rosy udders,
will not give their milk;

so the man who works the machine
dons cotton skirt, all floral delicate flounces
to hide his denim overalls and big old muddy boots,
he fastens the cool soft folds carefully,
wraps his head in his sweetheart's Sunday-best fringed scarf,
and walks smelling feminine and shy among the cows,

till the milk spurts, hot, slippery and steamy
into the churns,
Venus, Salome, Eve, and Fraulein Alberta
lowing, half-asleep,
accepting the disguised man as an echo of the woman,
their breath smelling of green, of milk's sweet traditional climax.

Hylda Sims

Gulf

Silence, empty as no man's dream

I'm a pink body hanging,
suspended in my baby colour;
am I born? Oh mother, let me be borne
on my cord, in this sapphire vacancy.

Blue. I'm tilting, turning, falling
in touchless, fruitless, birdless
say nothing, know nothing, be nothingness of blue, mother of all blue.

Arabian carpet dyed in shades of earth
floats up, flattens to a threadbare, faded brown
embossed with dunes, tracks, stones;
blueness retreats, holes up in the sky.

The distant hills are green

it is a perfect day on the plain
someone is playing a pipe
there are tents, no, tabernacles,
bells, long-legged, shaggy goats,
biblical, strolling with their keepers

a cloud of dust is moving towards me, gunfire
verily, even here. Trucks mirage from nowhere,
the ground shakes, rough ordering tongues...
One fighter down, alone; this is
the mother of all reality.

Ruth Smith

Close Quarters

It could have been designed by Wren.
We shake it out of its bag and slot
the jointed poles that raise it
into an apse. An opening
at either end admits us
to the nylon dome that fills
with northern light or holds its heat
under the high bake of a meseta sun.

Inside its lightweight walls
we've heard the sea,
thin cries from mountain birds
treefuls of sparrows, cracked
cathedral bells, infrequent trains,
a bullfrog all-nighter - and in the Alpujarras
once, two village clocks so out of synch
that midnight came round twice.

Each time we peg it down
to shallow-root it in another place
we disturb yesterday's dust
and shake from its folds red soil,
the blossom of olive trees, trapped
insects that have travelled here with us.
Going we leave behind, true measure
of ourselves, a double impress in the grass.

Margaret Speak

Lepus Timidus

The hare turned white
from eating snow, Pliny believed.
I've seen them buff in Spring
blue-grey in August, hiding
in blue shadows cast by rocks;
they have purity in cold light,
they impersonate the dead.
They only pair to mate
and guard their young.
Winter makes them solitary
like the broken-hearted girls
who died and assumed white hare shape.

She times her motherhood,
scrapes out a hollow on the moor,
one leveret, one form
to tease the predators
separate the scent;
not like this humming row
of incubators:
snuffles from the downy folds,
a wavering paw,
a quick, bright blink,
breath jagged as holly.

My pain of giving birth
was hot as the molten sun,
my daughter melded into me.
I'd tried not to let her go too soon
her skin had the pearly sheen
of mistletoe berries, the delicacy
of their faint green flesh

her legs splayed as the snow hare
poised for her zig zag flight.

Pauline Stainer

Walking the Tide-line on Ash Wednesday

Marginalia -
waters rewriting the landscape,
the wrack a deep fox-colour

velvet crabs in the eel-grass,
the sun slipping
its golden burnous

graveyards
shutting up the sea
with doors

a daylight moon
placing ashes
in a silver vessel

the lesser litany
of salt on shingle,
and further out

effleurage,
the hare's fur effect on glaze,
a killing in water.

Scarecrow

There's a man in the corn

Rest easy my dear

With red on his hands

Poppies my dear

He's crowned with storm-birds

Quickthorn my dear

I saw his face in the lightning's fork

Sockets clear my dear

The driven rain was the world's wide tear

Just so my dear

If I laid my eyes in, would you take him down?

O no my dear

The Plaster Room

Do not be deceived
By the hushed complexion of the room,
By the snow-moulded limbs.

Blanched disciplines abide here;
Medieval scissors hang on the wall,
Cages and casts, scrapers and cutters.

Patients filter in from the fracture clinic;
Green-stick children, supple as willow,
Their pliancy stilled under pallor.

Compound fractures from casualty,
The muted landscape of x-rays
Clipped to their stretchers.

The dying, with de-calcified bones,
The lace of their bodies
Beyond bone-setting.

The plasterer sluices his milky hands
Under the tap;
Caresses their effigies, like slip-ware -

With pure manipulation,
Sets a seal on their suffering
As in absolution.

The Divining of Wounds

O Mary, woe for his lying down
The priest cuts in the wax a cross;
we must put out the wounds by burning.

The body is a pierced vessel,
the flesh beeswax;
O Mary woe for his lying down

We divine from wounds
the stress of transcendence:
we must put out the wounds by burning.

Wounds draw: who are those
ranged round the anatomy theatre?
O Mary, woe for his lying down

The burning at Hiroshima
raised their arms like rushlights;
we must put out the wounds by burning.

Strike fire -
light a candle for the hallows.
O Mary, woe for his lying down
we must put out the wounds by burning.

The repeated line is taken from Lewis Glyn Cothi's On the Death of
His Son, *translated from the Welsh* (*Gwyn Williams,* The Burning
Tree).

Anne Stevenson

An Angel

After a long drive west into Wales,
as I lay on my bed, waiting
for my mind to seep back through my body,
I watched two gothic panels draw apart.
Between them loomed an angel,
tall as a caryatid, wingless.
draped like Michelangelo's sibyl.
Never have I felt so profoundly looked into.

She was bracing on her hip an immense book
that at first I took for a Bible. Then
prickling consciousness seemed to apprehend
The Recording Angel.
The pen she wielded writhed like a caduceus,
and on the book
ECCE LIBER MORI had been branded.

This book she held out towards me,
arm-muscles tensing, but even as I reached
I knew it was too heavy to hold.
Its gravity, she made me feel, would crush me,
a black hole of infinitely compressed time.
Each page weighed as much as the world.

Drawing my attention to a flaw in the book's crust -
a glazed porthole, a lens of alizarin -
she focused it (it must have been a microscope)
and silently motioned me to look.
Fire folding fire was all I saw. Then the red glass
cleared and a blizzard of swimming cells
swept underneath it, lashing their whip-like tails,
clashing, fusing, consuming each other greedily,
fountaining into polyps and underwater flowers.
Soon - fast-forward - forests were shooting up.
Seasons tamed lagoons of bubbling mud
where, hatching from the scum, animalculae

crawled, swarmed, multiplied, disbanded,
swarmed again, raised cities out of dust,
destroyed them, died. I turned to the angel,
'Save these species,' I cried.
And brought my face right down on her book,
my cheek on the lens like a lid.

Instantly I knew I had put out a light
that had never been generated by a book.
That vision-furnace, that blink into genesis?
Nothing but a passing reflection of the angel.

Rising, for the first time afraid,
I confronted her immortality
circling like a bracelet of phosphorus
just outside the windscreen of the car.
For it seems I was still driving.
Solidity and substance disappeared.
A noose of frenzied, shimmering electrons,
motes of an approaching migraine,
closed around me.
And through that fluorescent manacle,
the road flowed on through Wales.

Four and a Half Dancing Men

She knows how to fold
and turn the paper,
guiding the scissors with care
to create for her son
five little dancing dolls.
Toe by toe, hand in hand,
ring a ring a roses,
watch them caper

across the plain and up,
up over the mountain,
five happy men
to amuse a small boy in bed.
So cross. So bored. For
all that, a little blond god,
with the shifting realm
of his risen knees to govern.

The fauna buried in his
landslides, the cities
swallowed by his earthquakes
no longer divert him.
He monitors the marching
of five chained men
with silent intensity,
grave as his liquid eyes.

Up and down, up and down,
his to command,
one, two, three, four
manikins spring by.
He tears from the fifth
an arm, and then a thigh.
The troupe trips on,
though sagging at one end.

Four and a half dancing men.
And the half he made
with an act of his hand
seems to please him best.
He smiles. The same
can be done with the rest.
Four blind men, and a half,
unafraid, unafraid.

Leaving

Habits the hands have, reaching for this and that,
          (tea kettle, orange squeezer, milk jug,
          frying pan, sugar jar, coffee mug)
manipulate, or make, a habitat,
become its *genii loci,* working on
quietly in the kitchen when you've gone.

Objects a house keeps safe on hooks and shelves
          (climbing boots, garden tools, backpacks,
          bird feeders, tennis balls, anoraks)
the day you leave them bleakly to themselves,
do they decide how long, behind the door,
to keep your personality in store?

Good Bishop Berkeley made the objects stay
just where we leave them when we go away
by lending them to God. If so, God's mind
is crammed with things abandoned by mankind
          (featherbeds, chamber pots, flint lighters,
          quill pens, sealing wax, typewriters),

an archive of the infinitely there.
But there for whom? For what museum? And where?
I like to think of spiders, moths, white worms
leading their natural lives in empty rooms
          (egg-sacks, mouse-litter, dead flies,
          cobwebs, silverfish, small eyes)

while my possessions cease to study me
          (Emma, The Signet Shakespeare, Saving Whales,
          Living with Mushrooms, Leviathan, Wild Wales).
Habit by habit, they sink through time to be
one with the mind or instinct of the place,
home in its shadowy silence and stone space.

The White Room

Long summer shadows calm the grass,
each figure a finger.
Which ones are pointing to the past,
which to the future?

The tiny grey grandmother
loosens an immense shadow.
We shiver in it, but for her
it's a pontoon to the handsome fellow

she married - when was it
they honeymooned in the Philippines?
Teddy Roosevelt was President,
and he'd sent the marines

to educate the Filipinos; God
advancing with his stick.
And grandfather was Christian-good,
but he came home sick.

and the baby died; then money-troubles,
syphilis and silence as he sank
into the brass-locked, tissue-papered culls
of her steamer trunk.

How it hunches there, anchored hulk
in the surf of her candlewick bed cover
in the bride-white room we had to visit
with its incense of Bible-leather,
moth-balls and sweet unappeasable hurt.

In the Tunnel of Summers

Moving from day into day,
I don't know how,
eating these plums now
this morning for breakfast,
tasting of childhood's
mouth-pucker tartness,
watching the broad light
seed in the fences,
honey of barley,
gold ocean, grasses,
as the tunnel of summers,
of nothing but summers,
opens again
in my travelling senses.

I am eight and eighteen and eighty
all the Augusts of my day.

Why should I be, I be
more than another?
Brown foot in sandal,
burnt palm on flaked clay,
flesh under waterfall
baubled in strong spray,
blood on the stubble
of fly-sweet hay.
Why not my mother's my
grandmother's ankle
hurting as harvest hurts
thistle and animal?
A needle of burning;
why this way or that way?

They are already building the long straw cemetery
where my granddaughter's daughter has been born and buried.

Alicia Stubbersfield

Human Cannon-Ball

I am the closed hinge of myself
wedged in here, waiting for the word.
Outside there is the thickness of heat,
the stench of animals and almost silence.

I hear the tigers roar in the distance,
metal muffles everything until it stops
making sense and the only truth is here.
Cold touching my skin, seeping into me.

I have to stay small. I have to fit
inside this tube which goes on forever.
A circle of yellow above me,
my knees against my chest, fingers curled.

My father parades the ring,
leads the cannon so it is placed just so.
There is a net and I will land like a fish
scooped from water to be thrown back.

My flesh stays tight over bones
that flex and bend and give in
to his demands, his watching
when I eat: I mustn't grow too big.

Beyond this iron casing there is air,
animals loping backwards and forwards,
pegs hammered into rough grass
holding it all down.

He controls time and the force needed
to send me into that tremendous arc.
I stretch out for a moment, flying, flying
before the net clutches me: saved again.

Isobel Thrilling

Bending the Light

We are made from the raw
materials of space,
children of dust,
we carry reverberations,
fossilised light;
our elements never die.

Why do we navigate
life like
medieval mariners,
as if death were a ledge,
we drift
towards its rim?

Einstein in a carriage,
puzzled if passing trains
were moving or still,
discovered New Worlds,
saw the weight of the Earth
bending light.

Our perceptions
are always suspect,
who would care to deny
anti-matter
or the chemistry of angels?

Blood-Head

A head shaped from frozen
human blood shown
by Saatchi & Saatchi.

The woman on the radio
says it isn't red,
there are globules
that slip
into scarlet.

For days I've been haunted
by the grazed head
of the toddler
murdered by boys

and now this icon,

its dislocations from pity
and grief,
spilled blood
another kind of plasticine.

I await
the high-carat penis cut
from human urine;

the ultimate golden boy.

The Miner

The old miner grew
gooseberries;
gold and green
and bursting with sunlight.

He trained
unlikely butterflies
of sweet-pea;
his allotment was an oasis
of cabbages and beans.

At home
his helmet stood in its
usual place.
It had held his thoughts,
protected his vision
of sky and soil
when he fought the darkness.

He still touched it
with respect;
a piece of rare armour.

On Blindness

Darkness:
constellations of shadow,
black moons at noon;

I learned new maps,
white space
that grew a landscape
from cadence,
trees and birds,
huge thunderheads of leaves.

Gardens
became amorphous,
breath jagged
with volts from lilac and pine:
a barbed
diffusion of roses.

My blind friend in the ward
told how light
had collapsed one morning,
she spoke of sun,
handling the thought for gold.

A needlewoman once,
now sound became her silk,
she wove her days,
visions still rooted
in hollyhocks
and cottage plots.

I lay,
my eyelids stitched.
Would life lose
scarlet, vermilion, red?

Words slowly
acquired the potency of blood.

Val Warner

from: Tooting Idyll

Dust

1.

Even the cabbage white's surrender flag
flapping across forget-me-nots, heart's-ease,
across the close June garden day...till all
the colours fade...reminds me: two years back,
sweeping the years' dust from your room, that first
time in this other life - pupating time -
I found it on the floorboards' black-stained fringe
around the foot-loose carpet. Flashier
than any brooch, filigreed red on black
- a little touch of hearth-light in the night?
Butterfly wing - Red Admiral? - its pair
pure dust. I left it on the window-sill:
the sun that lit its flittering, quick day
would quickly grind its pigments, too, to dust.
A sombre gesture, maybe . . . lighting our
luck beyond chance, till history end luck.
Or we fall through the garden's light-veiled ice.

2.

Together, we worshipped that butterfly
wing's filigree of *le rouge et le noir.*
'Darwin spoilt that, as token of our life
after life.' '*Would* you have believed, before . . .?'
'*Would* you . . . believing Paley? Dear God -' 'Who

knows in another life, another time
and place . . . the old watchmaker's hand transpired?'
Reincarnation, resurrection, Jove
- we shuffled menus from shut restaurants.
'Even in death' - that flutter-by - 'it's fine,
unlike us.' Even then, vivacious mites
nibbled through . . . 'what the eye can't see?' We stared

at that wing's Cyclops' eye, ground of dried blood.
Evolved through mud to grub, through dust to dust...
because you had responded, it became
more than a pretty thing I'd seen: our eyes
ricocheted off that wing's ripe edge, that tear.

Susan Wicks

Persephone

Wanting someone who looked natural,
they cast you as Persephone, not thinking
how at regular intervals you were taken
to visit your own mother
under a flaking sky of cream paint
down the echoing corridor
to the long-stay ward, where trees
froze in the black glass
of winter - how you were no stranger
to the clockwork rhythms of figures
moaning and swaying, the mechanical
hands that moved across faces
or scattered things in odd corners,
the hungry hands that flapped after
with their wings of ragged knitting.
Each time you would leave her and return
to birdsong, the urgent green
through frost, the melting grass, the world
you would give her if she would only
recognise you through the heavy doors
your father closed between you. Each week
you rehearsed your flower-steps
with a basket of paper petals
as your teachers smiled down on you, exclaiming
at your sweet face,
at the way you seemed never to see him coming -
as if each last dance were the first dance,
and every mother won over by so little.

Monet : The Chicago Haystacks

It has taken us years to create
this palimpsest: haystacks pregnant with light,
these shadow-skirts belling
towards onlookers. Now we have surrendered
our coats, our back-packs, our tweed
headgear. Our necks no longer remember
zips, the snap collars of down jackets:
now there is nothing between us
but a plastic chip. Your fruit-shimmer
becomes our breathing, your snow
melts for us; your sharp stalks
write on our cold faces. In layers of light
the mottled stack reclothes itself.
Our eyes blink back ghosts, our fingers close
on air. Leaving our shuttered lenses,
our Walkmans' coiled umbilicals
of flex, our shiny packages, we have reached
into light, snow, haystacks. Our bare hands
rifle you, topple your ricks
with inept stokes, as we roll together
in interior dark. We look at you. We shimmer
with death, rose, winter, peeling you
to see one another.

Merryn Williams

Blood Donor

It all floats back. I'm staring at the ceiling,
as others queue, to give blood for Vietnam;
tense as a cat, deliberately ignoring
the scarlet trickle leaking from my arm.
I see you stand up, taller than all the others,
stagger, somebody guides you to a bed;
stare through the crowd, my interest never wavers,
trained hard on you - but *touch me not*, you'd said.
The capsule cracks; high windows, August heat,
me lying on the white unspotted sheet.

There's no real sequel. All those students scattered,
some dead. Vietnam stopped bleeding long ago.
I turn the page; my son becomes an adult,
walks those same streets, the age and height of you.
In dreams, I feel the needle scratch my wrist,
and think of blood, our blood that never mixed.

Wilfred's Bridge

November 1st, 1998

Shrewsbury flooded. Three of the four roads
out of town blocked, and the Severn steadily rising,
drowning alders, swamping riverside gardens.
Water has wholly cut off the Welsh Bridge;
the English Bridge you can still wade over, on duckboards.
Water enters the little shops, boutiques
and newsagents, seeps into the big wine warehouse
on London Road, and bottles are washed from their cellars,
carried out on the tide. On Wilfred's bridge,
you stand and watch them bob along with sticks
and froth, in brief bursts of November light,
giving the dark brown liquid a richer taste,
dirtying the foam. The stream is travelling past
the Norman sandstone abbey, Wilfred's church.
He isn't here. His body is in France.

His name came back, is written on a tablet
high on its walls.

He never mentioned Shrewsbury.
To him it was reactionary, provincial;
like most young kids, he couldn't wait to get out.
Yet, this weekend, his picture is all over
the town. It's eighty years since Wilfred caught
that train; you still see SHREWSBURY on the white
illuminated name-plates, as he saw them.
Still there, the blood-red abbey. And still here,
the swollen Severn. Timbered houses pulled down
and towers put up, but still, he'd know this place.

I close my eyes. I call him back. His words
from a discarded manuscript - *What though
we sink from men as pitchers falling, many
shall raise us up.* I see him, in a crowd
of boys and girls, streaming out of the Technical School
- now swept away - that stood on the English bank;
sixteen, a smooth-cheeked student, carrying
his poetry textbooks under one arm, walking
across the river.

When the floods recede
they'll leave a legacy of dirt, soaked deep
into the fabric. Rubbish, fallen leaves
and cardboard cartons, human waste, floats down,
choking the wells, as he wrote home from France.
This ancient bridge rebuilt and widened, using
the same stones, Wilfred's generation gone -
or carrying wounds round with them, which don't bleed.
Water, from Wales and England, hurrying past
the bursting arches, tidemarks long submerged,
so we can't see them, as we cross the stream.
The rubbish forming floating islands, which
the current pushes, finds its own way through.

Frances Wilson

Making Poppy Dolls

Finding them's easy - the excitement's
in the heat of the long afternoon, the smell
of tar - because they're common enough,
shove their way between ranks of orderly corn
at the field's edge, line up along roadsides,
flaunting scarlet. They're asking to be picked.

But once you're down in the sour grass
beside them you see they're fragile, teetering
on tall stalks, their silk still creased -
mothwings emerging. For a second you pause before,
choosing the brightest, you fumble your fingers
right down where it's dark, to snap it off low.

Now it gets tricky. There's no way your sweat
won't do damage as you fold back each tissue petal
and pinch them tight into a neat waist so that the top
rounds out into a pert bust; as you twist the wide grass
sash to hold it all firm, taking pains with the knot
so that the blade won't break, leaving the head

exposed in its soft ruff. Now you want something
sharp, a few quick jabs, to prick the features.
Next, for a second leg, take a length of stem
and poke it up under the skirt, another through
the bodice for the arms, even if they always look
crucified, the eyes terrified, the mouth howling.

It could always be singing. Only it isn't.
And there's nothing you can do except lay them
in rows. Even the fizz of the wind through dry corn
won't lift their skirts now. And you're bored,
with nothing to show but dead flowers and red
smears on your fingers. And wishing you hadn't.

Coming of Age

Like boys at the first windfall
of conkers, spiders at the first frisson
of autumn, this June day's midsummer
sunshine has brought you out: old women

risking pastels, blatantly barelegged -
you, whose grandson years ago stuck up
my daughter's hair with playdough -
you, who used to drive me round

for Meals on Wheels, and knew each
name but always called me 'Florence' -
in shorts even! How you brazen out
aging, exposing varicose wirings,

melting ankles, bird-legs; how you dress up
your crowning glory's lack-lustre
with wild hats or dyeing or just waving.
Straight backed, defiantly driving,

or blocking access with zimmers,
shopping trolleys - inexorable as tanks,
you get your own back on skateboarders,
those youths who at night darken your doorways.

I'm not one of you yet, but as I wait behind
you in queues, you already acknowledge me
differently, recognise marking: the backs
of my hands, how I stand against sunlight.

And I catch your private humming, pick up
a sweetish brittle scent of something folded
inward; half glimpse beyond smudged lipstick,
runnels of eyeshadow, your small fierce glances,

your reedy intimacies, your painful optimism -
things I've also known and dreamed of, never told.
A kind of pollen count. O bright, brave,
indomitable old women, I'm coming, I'm coming.

Understanding Rodin

In the afternoon art class
we're drawing each other.
Women who've come with friends
move closer together. In a corner
a fat man shrinks behind his easel.
His gratitude as I settle beside
him is humbling, how he offers
himself, shoulders awkward, shyly.

Just a faint scratch as charcoal
explores ears, coils into nostrils,
approaches the neat indentation
above his upper lip where my finger
would fit. Where the lips touch,
how private that line between closed
and open, how lovely this slack
curve's soft edge, his mouth.

And I understand Rodin, why he made
love to his models, having known them
in stone. Not to would have been
far more unfeeling. And no wonder
they went mad, wrote to him daily,
arranged the rooms where they waited
in pastels subtle as flesh for that
slow discovery of their own beauty.

Dilys Wood

Horace's Seventh Ode

We've been translating Horace, who says
that, if you filmed the year and ran it fast,
icicles would become glittered heels
of Spring-renewing streams, green shades projected
would fall as brown leaves, sink to the bottom
when ice stole out from the banks, darkened the flow.
To me, Horace is a Roman fragment.
Horace is more to you, a fascinating
virile professor, father substitute -
you strive to be our Horace's best girl.

Friday Fish Man

'Walking up the street,
the man whose brother killed their father'

Who do we forgive in circumstance unknown?

We forgive you for dying - hard as that is -
no flesh on you, fish or fowl, despite feeding,
breasts like buttoned pockets
on a dress shrunk around your shoulders,
stomach hugely swollen with tumours.

With your stick in play,
hand linked in my arm,
we walk up the street to meet your new friend,
friend of the dying,
fish man with a single Shakespeare gold-earring.

Neck like a bull, he does Friday nights
as Night-Club bouncer.

You are one of those
whose world keels over
more often than not.
              The fish man,
reliable, leaves Hastings at 6 a.m.
provides the week in fridge or freezer -
makes dying easier, tickles your tongue
with Finnan Haddock, cleaver on the table.

He says to eat Dabs
before they die on us -
'Today, tomorrow, or freeze the lot'

O.K. . . . there's the morose neighbour
again. We clutch our parcels tightly.

'All are brothers of men who killed their fathers'

Who do we forgive in circumstance unknown?

Go to the fish man, suck forgiveness from his bones.

Lynne Wycherley

Tawny Owl

The first time I met you, I was walking
on a hillside. You were a sculpture
in the cleft of a tree, waiting for
the sky to shut its yellow flower.

The leaves were a shaman's rattle
in the wind's dry mouth.
You peered at me from dreaming depths,
fawn barbules silking your body.

That night I thought of you
turning your head like a radar dish,
huge eyes in a Hallowe'en face
probing our shells, seeing

each loneliness, each twisting
gut of grief. I pictured the pulse
of your wings, softer and slower
than the systoles of our hearts

as you orbit like Pluto, patrolling
the edge of known and unknown
to alight on a blood-drop,
your talons spreading to a cross.

Each year I hear the bone-flute
of your voice, hooked beak
blowing through a hole in stone,
calling the faint stars closer

calling who? who? who?
Your question hollows our mirrors.
The moon passes our windows
searching each face.

When I am old, I will step with
the Navaho through the cavern
of your voice. I will dress my bent body
in a shawl of chestnut feathers.

I will glimpse the night as never before:
cyan, hyaline, infra-red.
I will swallow my brief life
and wrap its bones in velvet

my thighs will turn to tarsars,
the horizon will shrink
to an astonished O
as my shoulder-blades open to the stars.

Biographical Notes

ANNA ADAMS had several pamphlets published by Headland in the early 70s. Her first collection was *A Reply to Intercepted Mail* (Peterloo Poets, 1979). *Green Resistance, New and Selected Poems*, was published by Enitharmon Press in 1996. Her fifth book from Peterloo Poets, *Flying Underwater*, is due 2002/2003. She is at present finalising an anthology of London poems and prose, to follow *Thames* (Enitharmon Press, 1999) her anthology of poems about the river Thames. She has also published two prose books, *Island Chapters* (Littlewood Press, 1991) and *Life on Limestone* (Smith Settle, 1993).

FLEUR ADCOCK has published eleven books of poetry and edited anthologies, including *The Faber Book of Twentieth Century Women's Poetry*. She has translated collections by two Romanian poets, as well as a book of medieval Latin poems, *The Virgin and the Nightingale* (Bloodaxe). She has received several awards, including a Cholmondeley Award (1976), a New Zealand National Book Award in 1984, and an OBE in 1996. She lives in London. Her most recent collection is *Poems 1960-2000* (Bloodaxe, 2000).

GILLIAN ALLNUTT Her latest collection, *Lintel* (Bloodaxe, 2001) was a Poetry Book Society Choice and was shortlisted for the T S Eliot Prize. Her previous Collection, *Nantucket and the Angel* (Bloodaxe, 1997) was also shortlisted for the T S Eliot Prize, and she has published three other collections, *Spitting the Pips Out* (Sheba, 1981) *Beginning the Avocado* (Virago, 1987) and *Blackthorn* (Bloodaxe, 1994). She is the author of *Berthing: A Poetry Workbook* (NEC / Virago, 1991), co-editor of *The New British Poetry* (Paladin, 1988) and formerly the poetry editor of *City Limits*. She lives in County Durham.

MONIZA ALVI was born in Pakistan in 1954 and grew up in Hertfordshire. Her first two collections, *The Country at My Shoulder* and *A Bowl of Warm Air* were published by OUP. *Carrying My Wife* (Bloodaxe, 2000) was a Poetry Book Society Recommendation. Her latest collection is *Souls* (Bloodaxe, 2002). She says, "Writing poetry has enabled me to explore and come to terms with the difficulties and pleasures of growing up as a girl with a racially mixed background. I am pleased that there are some marvellous women writers with multi-cultural backgrounds who have inspired me and who will be there for the poets of the future".

R.V. BAILEY lives in Gloucestershire. She was born in Northumberland, educated at Whitley Bay Grammar School, Girton College, Cambridge and St Anne's College, Oxford. "I wrote poetry as a student; began writing seriously later because I had to teach students creative writing and they wouldn't let me get away without joining in..." Her first collection is *Course Work* (Culverhay Press, 1997). She reviews for *The North* and *Envoi* and has given poetry readings with U.A. Fanthorpe, whose poetry Audiotapes, *Double Act* (Penguin) and *Poetry Quartets 5* (Bloodaxe) include Bailey's voice.

JILL BAMBER began to write in her 40s, "mostly at night when the children were asleep." She has 5 books published - the latest is *Flying Blind*, published by the National Poetry Foundation. She was twice winner of the London Writers Competition and Blue Nose Poet of the Year in 1997-8. Her collections are available in Braille and print from the National Poetry Library and from the RNIB.

WENDY BARDSLEY has taught widely. Whilst working in the Manchester Inspection and Advisory Service for Education, she was responsible for matters concerning the United Nation Convention for the Rights of the Child and has been on radio and television. She is a literary critic and writes poetry for adults, young people and children. She has published four poetry collections, two anthologies and works of non-fiction for use in education. Her fourth collection is *Solving Atlantis* (Headland, 2002).

WANDA BARFORD lives in London. She was born in Milan in the Mussolini era and emigrated as a child to Zimbabwe. "I studied music at the Royal College but my first love was literature, particularly poetry. Compelled to earn a living teaching the piano, I did not put poetry in the centre of my life until my late-50s". She has been widely published in magazines, anthologies, and national newspapers. Her two collections from Flambard Press are, *Sweet Wine and Bitter Herbs* and *A Moon at the Door*. A third, *Losing, Finding*, is forthcoming. Working with *The Holocaust Educational Trust* and using her poetry about the Holocaust, she goes into schools to give seminars to older children.

ELIZABETH BARTLETT lives in West Sussex. "To me poetry is a vocation. I left grammar school at 15. My first poem was published by *Poetry London* when I was 18. I did not have a collection published until I was 55, when Harry Chambers of Peterloo invited me to send. *A Lifetime of Dying* was published. I am now mid-70s and still writing". *Two Women Dancing, New and Selected Poems* (Bloodaxe, 1995) was followed by *Appetites of Love* (Bloodaxe, 2001).

JACQUELINE BARTLETT lives in Heswall in the Wirral. Her poetry has been published in magazines, in the Canadian Mekler-Deahl Anthology 2000 and has been broadcast on BBC Radio Merseyside. She has also published short fiction and children's short-stories. She has worked as a creative writing tutor for WEA and is co-ordinator of Wordscapes, a poets' monthly workshop.

JANE BEESON was a painter until 1970, studying at the Slade, and exhibiting in the Arnolfini Gallery, Bristol, in London (various galleries), Sheffield, Leeds, Liverpool, Hull amongst other places. In 1973, she switched her career to writing. Her poetry has appeared in numerous magazines and anthologies, including *New Poetry 5* and *6*, published by Arts Council/ Hutchinson and many editions of *New Poetry*, ed. Norman Hidden. She has been read on Radio 3 and 4. She has published four novels and also writes plays for TV and Radio. She has two poetry collections published by Headland, *Imago*, 1987 and *Quartz*, 1997.

ANNE BERESFORD has published 12 collections of poetry, the first in 1967. Her *Selected and New Poems* was published by Agenda Editions and Bellow Publishing, 1997 and her latest, *No Place for Cowards* by Katabasis, 1998. She grew up in London and now lives in Suffolk. She is married and has three children and five grandchildren.

ELIZABETH BEWICK Born in Co. Durham, she has lived in Winchester for the past forty years. She is active in poetry circles in the city and runs a small all-women writers' workshop from her cottage. She has been writing poetry all her life but only seriously considered publication in retirement. Her first book, *Comfort Me With Apples*, was published in a limited edition in 1987, illustrated with wood-engravings by the publisher, Graham Williams, at the Florin Press. *Heartsease*, her first full collection, was published by Peterloo Poets in 1991, followed by *Making a Roux* from the same publisher in 2000.

PATRICIA BISHOP lives in Gloucestershire. She has been widely published in magazines and anthologies. For 5 years she was poet in residence to Penwith libraries. In addition to minor prizes, she came second in the 1994 National Poetry Competition, won an Arts Council/BBC award which involved reading her poems on Radio 3 and more recently won a Arts Council/Cotswold DC Artist of the Year Award. Her publications include, *Double Exposure* (Westwords) and *Aubergine is a Gravid Woman* (Headland). Her third and fourth collections are *Saving Dragons* (2000) and *Time's Doppleganger* (2002), both from Oversteps Books.

ANNE BORN lives in South Devon. She has 12 collections of which the latest is *Planting Light*, Headland, 1999. "Early marriage, university and children took up most time until my fourth and last child was three, but poetry has always been of the greatest importance in my professional life. I work as a full-time literary translator, mainly of fiction but also of poetry". She is a Reader and reviewer of Scandinavian books, leads poetry workshops for all ages and her imprint, Oversteps Books, publishes (by invitation only) one or two titles a year.

PAT BORTHWICK lives in Yorkshire and started to write poetry later in life. She has published one full-length collection, *Between Clouds and Caves* (Littlewood Press, 1989) and four further pamphlets (Pharos Press). She has twice been awarded a Yorkshire Arts Writers Bursary and, most recently a YA Artists Award. She is part-time tutor in Creative Writing at Leeds University. She devised and co-organises the Yorkshire Open Poetry Competition.

JACQUELINE BROWN lives near Sheffield in the Hope Valley. "Born in 1944 in West Yorkshire, I began writing as a child of five - academic work then took over and it was not until the early 1980's that I began writing seriously. Poetry is not easy. It requires a dive into the inner self which can sometimes be disturbing, but there is nothing to beat the feeling of having produced something new and as perfect as one can make it." Her collections include, *Accidental Reality* (Littlewood Press) *Thinking Egg*, winner of the Arvon/Observer prize and *In a Woman's Likeness* (a Poetry Book Society Recommendation) - the last two were published by Arc Publications.

NADINE BRUMMER lives and writes in London and Dorset. "I was born in Manchester to Jewish parents - the first from a large extended family to go to university, winning an exhibition to Somerville. Illness prevented me completing Greats at Oxford. Later, I took a Philosophy Degree at Birkbeck College, University of London. After several years as a psychiatric social worker, I was appointed lecturer and Tutor at Goldsmiths College. Writing poetry came late. My first published poem was in *New Poetry 4*, PEN / Hutchison. A first chapbook collection, *A Question of Blue Tulips and Other Poems* (Shoestring Press, 1999) was followed by publication in a wide range of magazines, including *London Magazine* and *Poetry London*."

CATHERINE BYRON "I was born in 1947 and grew up in Belfast, child of an English father and a Southern Irish mother. I studied medieval literature at Somerville. My mongrel inheritance lay dormant until my late 30s, when insistent dreams summoned me to the West of Ireland to write *Galway*, a sequence based on my grandmother's life (Settlements 1985 and 1993). I have recently written about my parents' mixed marriage in 'The Most Difficult Door' (Women's Lives Into Print, ed. P. Polkey, Macmillan, 1999)." In 1997 she received an ACE Writer's Award. In 2001 she was invited to India to give talks, readings and lectures on the creative link between her work as a web or wired poet for the Poetry Society and her on-going work in print, especially *The Getting of Vellum* (Salmon/Blackwater, 2000).

SALLY CARR lives in Wiltshire. "Writing is my way of making some sense of life. I started writing when my children were small as something I could do while they were asleep or at playschool. I had previously taught poetry. I won the Bridport prize in 1993 with a poem which was the direct upshot of a traumatic time in family life. I have had more than 80 poems published in magazines and anthologies. It took a long time and a hard slog to reach the milestone of a first collection - many editors saw my poems as 'too quiet', 'too domestic'." Her first collection is *Electrons on Bonfire Night* (Rockingham Press, 1997). A second, *Handing on the Genes*, is due from Rockingham, 2002.

LIZ CASHDAN "I teach Creative Writing at Sheffield University. Two shared publications from Smith/Doorstop are *Troublesome Cattle* and *Almost Like Talking*. The most recent is *Laughing All The Way* (Five Leaves, 1995). I started writing when a secondary school English teacher and realised that I couldn't teach writing without being a writer. Just now I am doing some research into women writers of the Romantic period - 300 women poets in print in 1800 and even more novelists and travel writers."

ALISON CHISHOLM lives in Merseyside where she works as a poetry and creative writing tutor. "Poetry has been at the heart of my life since my very early teens, first as a spoken art to gain qualifications in speech and drama, then as the best medium for thoughts and feelings." She writes on poetry for *Writers' News, Writing, Springboard, Freelance Market News*, and her writer's guides, *The Craft of Writing Poetry* and *A Practical Writing Course* are published by Allison & Busby. Winner of the 2001 Wells Literature Festival International Poetry Competition. Her latest collection is *Daring The Slipstream* (Headland, 1997).

GILLIAN CLARKE was born in Cardiff of Welsh-speaking parents. She has published 7 collections of poetry. Her work is studied for the GCSE and A level in England and Wales. She teaches on the Creative Writing M.Phil course at the University of Glamorgan. Recent collections of poems include *Collected Poems* (Carcanet,1997) and *Five Fields* (Carcanet, 1998) and a collection for children, *The Animal Wall and Other Poems* (Pont Books, 1999). She lives in Ceredigion.

ANNE CLUYSENAAR, daughter of the painter John Cluysenaar, was born in Belgium. Graduate (1957) of Trinity College, Dublin and an Irish citizen, she lives on a smallholding in South Wales. She is a consultant in creative writing at the University of Wales, Cardiff, takes writing workshops and edits the journal *Scintilla*. She has written songs and the verse text for a Millennium son-et-lumiere at Tintern Abbey. Her new and selected poems, *Timeslips* (Carcanet, 1997) contained 'Vaughan Variations', evoking the life and work of the poet Henry Vaughan. Anne is now exploring the relationship between scientific discovery and spiritual insight through poems on natural history dedicated to the memory of the Usk-born naturalist Alfred Russel Wallace, co-discoverer with Darwin of natural selection and father of biogeography.

GLADYS MARY COLES Her nine collections include *The Echoing Green* (Flambard, 2001). *The Glass Island* (1992) and *Leafburners: New & Selected Poems* (1986), both from Duckworth. Her poetry is anthologised by Faber, Virago, Collins, Seren, and Forward, and was selected for *Poems of the Decade, 1992-2001* (Forward, 2001). She has edited seven anthologies, including *The Poet's View: Poems for Paintings* (1996). The winner of numerous poetry competitions, she has received a Welsh Arts Council Writer's Award and the Daily Post Arts Award for Literature/Writing. Radio work includes a BBC Radio Four 'Kaleidoscope' Special Feature. She is the authority on writer Mary Webb, with two acclaimed biographies and editions of Webb's poetry and prose. A lecturer in Poetry and Creative Writing at both Liverpool University and Liverpool John Moores University, she has led courses for Arvon and the Taliesin Trust (Tŷ Newydd).

WENDY COPE was born in Kent and took her degree at St Hilda's College, Oxford. After university, she worked for 15 years as a primary-school teacher in London. Her first collection, *Making Cocoa for Kingsley Amis* (Faber and Faber, 1986, a Poetry Book Society Recommendation) established her at once as a widely-read poet. In 1987 she received a Cholmondeley Award for Poetry. She has published since, *Twiddling Your Thumbs* (for children), *The River Girl, Serious Concerns* and *If I Don't Know* (Faber, 2001).

ELSA CORBLUTH lives near Weymouth in Dorset. She is published in many anthologies, poetry magazines and journals and has two collections from Peterloo Poets, *St. Patrick's Night* (1988) and *The Planet Iceland* (2002). Her many prizes for poetry include the National and Arvon Competitions. Her poems have been broadcast on Radios 3 and 4.

TRICIA COROB used to teach literature, creative writing and theatre studies for colleges of higher and further education, including Birkbeck. In the 1980s, she made the first of several extended visits to India, living and working with teachers of the ancient tradition of Advaita Vedanta. Since then, she has been leading workshops which combine Eastern and Western approaches to personal development. Her poems have been published in magazines and anthologies and her first collection, *House of Tides* was published by Mosaic Press in 1997.

HILARY DAVIES is Head of Languages at St. Paul's Girls' School. "I began writing poetry only after a degree in French/German at Oxford. While a post-graduate, I founded the magazine *Argo*. I won a Gregory Award 1983 and the TLS/Cheltenham Festival poetry competition in 1987, with a Hawthornden Fellowship in 1992. My subject matter is not female-oriented and I attach no particular significance to being a woman. Some critics have called me 'intellectual', 'academic', 'metaphysical', 'religious'- depending on your point of view, this is a judgment of praise or opprobrium." Collections are: *The Shanghai Owner Of The Bonsai Shop*, 1991 and *In A Valley Of This Restless Mind*, 1996, both Enitharmon Press. Recently, *Acumen Poetry Magazine* published part of her sonnet-sequence, *The Dismembered Spirit*.

ANGELA DOVE lives in London where she works as a museums education consultant, teacher and writer. She studied Theatre Design and Acting and went on to a career in the theatre, followed by teaching Performance Arts at Middlesex University. In 1998 she and her partner established Poetry Works and the Cats Night Out series of Readings at the Poetry Cafe which promote contemporary women's poetry. "I came to writing both early and late with a big gap in between. Writing was very important to me as a child but then I went in a different direction . . . I began to write again at a crucial time about four years ago when struggling to come to terms with a difficult childhood." She has been widely published in poetry magazines and anthologies, including *Poetry Review, Poetry London, Thumbscrew* and the Enitharmon/Second Light anthology, *Parents*.

JANE DURAN was born in Cuba in 1944. Brought up in the United States and in Chile, she has lived in England since 1966. A pamphlet of her poems, *Boogie Woogie*, was published by Hearing Eye in 1991 and a selection of her work appeared in *Poetry Introduction 8* (Faber and Faber, 1993). Her first full collection, *Breathe Now, Breathe* (Enitharmon Press, 1995) won the 1995 Forward Prize for Best First Collection. Her second collection, *Silences from the Spanish Civil War*, is also published by Enitharmon, 2002.

JEAN EARLE, who died recently, lived near Shrewsbury. "I published stories and poetry (of a lighter kind) in my 20s with a good deal of journalism with short radio pieces. After marriage and children somehow it all vanished - but not owing to domesticity, I simply lost the urge. In my late 60s this returned in a flood, now relating to poetry of quite a different kind - so urgent that it quite possessed me. I published my first collection, *A Trial of Strength* (Carcanet, 1980) when I was 71. I have not found any masculine or feminine significance in my writing simply my own way of looking." *Visiting Light* (Poetry Wales Press, 1987) was a Poetry Book Society Choice. Her *Selected Poems*, 1990, *The Sun in the West*, 1995 and *The Bed of Memory*, 2001, are published by Seren.

CHRISTINE EVANS She has lived and worked in Wales for over thirty years. Both her collections of poetry, *Cometary Phases* and *Island of Dark Horses* are published by Seren Books. She is one of four contributors to *A Year in a Small Country* (Gomer Press).

RUTH FAINLIGHT's eleventh collection of poems, *Sugar-paper Blue* (Bloodaxe, 1997) was shortlisted for the Whitbread Prize. She has also published 2 collections of short stories, translations from Portugese and Spanish and written libretti for the Royal Opera House and Chanel 4 TV. In 1994 she received the Cholmondeley Award for Poetry. Her latest Collection is *Burning Wire* (Bloodaxe, 2002).

U. A. FANTHORPE lives in Gloucestershire. She read English at Oxford and went on to become Head of English at Cheltenham Ladies College. She decided to try to be a writer in 1971. Her first collection, *Side Effects*, 1978, was followed by five others from Peterloo Poets. In 1986 King Penguin published *Selected Poems* (published as a hard-back by Peterloo), in 1998 came *Double Act*, a Penguin audiobook with R.V. Bailey, and in 2000 *Consequences*, Peterloo. In 1994 she was the first woman nominated for the post of Professor of Poetry at Oxford. Carol Ann Duffy has said of her work, "U A Fanthorpe is a popular poet - reprinted, studied in schools . . . [she has] done much to make poetry accessible . . . able to write deceptively simple poems which enable us to recognise ourselves."

ELAINE FEINSTEIN lives in London. She says, "Writing has been essential to my emotional survival. I have lived as a writer since 1980." She is a poet and novelist and her versions of the Russian poet Marina Tsvetayeva's poetry have recently been re-issued from Carcanet/OUP. In 1990 she received a Cholmondeley Award for poetry. In 1995 she was the Chairman of Judges for the T. S. Eliot prize. Her *Selected Poems* was published in 1994 by Carcanet. *Daylight* (Carcanet 1997) was a Poetry Book Society Recommendation. Her latest collection is *Gold* (Carcanet, 2000.) She recently published a biography of Pushkin (Weidenfeld and Nicholson) and edited *After Pushkin, Versions by Contempoary Poets* for the Folio Society. Her biography of Ted Hughes, *Ted Hughes, The Life of a Poet* was published, Weidenfeld and Nicolson, 2001.

KATE FOLEY lives in Amsterdam and Suffolk. "Early start in writing, aged 11, late start in publication, aged 55. In between, midwife, teacher and a career in conservation leading to the headship of national archeological science / conservation laboratory. As someone thoroughly imbued with feminist / Lesbian / and now 'grey' issues, I naturally see myself as a 'woman writer' with all that implies both of strength and practical disadvantages. But I can't write a p.c. poem to save my life . . ." Her collections are *Soft Engineering* (Onlywomen Press, 1994) and *A Year Without Apricots* (Blackwater Press, 2000).

WENDY FRENCH works in a psychiatric hospital with adolescents suffering from mental health problems. She is currently researching for a Ph.D connections between mental health and creativity in the life and work of the poet and composer Ivor Gurney. Her poems have been published in magazines and anthologies.

KATHERINE FROST lives in London. "I may be the last generation of women for whom seriously delayed entry to poetry-writing is the rule. Let us hope so. I proclaimed myself a future poet at 7 but recovered the thread only in middle life....Workshops have been important in developing confidence....." She was the winner of the 1994 Poetry Business Competition and her first collection, *The Sixth Channel* is published by Smith / Doorstop (1995). She has been widely published in poetry magazines and anthologies, including *Poetry London, Poetry Review, Wild Cards: the Second Virago Anthology of Writing Women* (Virago, 1999) and in *Scanning the Century: the Penguin Book of the Twentieth Century in Poetry* (Viking / The Poetry Society, 1999). She was one of 11 writers anthologised in *Tying the Song, A First Anthology from the Poetry School*, Enitharmon Press, 2000.

CYNTHIA FULLER was born in Kent but has lived in the North East since the 1970s working freelance as a teacher of literature and creative writing in Adult and Higher education. She was one of the editors of *Writing Women*, an important outlet for women's poetry supported in the 1980s and 1990s by Virago Press. She has three collections of poetry, all published by Flambard Poetry, *Moving Towards Light* (1992), *Instructions for the Desert* (1996), *Only A Small Boat* (2001).

ANNE-MARIE FYFE was born in Cushendall on the Antrim Coast and now lives with her husband and two children in London. She teaches literature and creative writing and runs the *Coffee House Poetry Reading* series at *The Troubadour* in Earl's Court. *Late Crossing*, her first collection, was published by Rockingham in 1999, followed by *Tickets from a Blank Window*, also published by Rockingham. Both collections include many poems reflecting on her Northern Ireland up-bringing.

KATHERINE GALLAGHER is Australian born and now lives in London. She is a widely published poet, translator and poetry tutor. "I started writing poetry in 1965, encouraged by the burgeoning women's movement with its poetry anthologies and new publishing outlets for women. Poetry has become my life, my way of seeing. In our era, the fight for visibility is common to all poets but it presents special difficulties for women. There's one answer - and that is to keep writing." Her collection *Passengers to the City* (Hale and Iremonger, 1985) was shortlisted for the 1986 Australian National Poetry Prize. Other collections are, *Fish-Rings on Water* (Forest Books, 1989), a pamphlet, *Finding the Prince* (Hearing Eye, 1993) and *Tigers on the Silk Road* (Arc, 2000).

PAMELA GILLILAN who lived in Bristol, sadly died while this anthology was in preparation. She said of her late start as a writer, "Wonderful to have achieved late in life an ambition cherished as a child. Writing regained importance after a long interval - about 25 years - during which I neither read nor wrote poetry but was absorbed in other forms of creativity. In 1977 I suddenly knew that I'd be able to write again, but found that my poems were very different . . . I sent poems to Competitions as they'd be judged anonymously. This was in 1979, when I had successes in the Cheltenham and the Poetry Society Competitions. I'm sure that this led directly to publication with Bloodaxe of my first book, *That Winter*. Three more followed from Bloodaxe - my latest, *The Rashomon Syndrome*, 1998".

ANN GRAY lives in Cornwall. Her first collection was *Painting Skin* (Fatchance Press, 1995). There followed a collaboration, *Gronw's Stone* (Headland, 1997) and a second collection, *The Man I Was Promised* (Headland, 2002). Her poems have been set to music, danced to and have been read on radio. They appeared in the 1995 *Forward Anthology*.

CATHY GRINDROD lives in Derbyshire. Until recently she was the Editor of *Poetry Nottingham International* and is now Literature Development Officer for Nottingham City. "I did not begin writing poetry until 8 years ago at the age of 32. Until then, life, responsibilities and children came first, although poetry had been an absorbing interest from an early age. Now the writing, teaching and promoting of poetry has taken over my life." She is widely published in magazines, with a collection, *Something the Heart Can't hold*, published by the Nottingham Poetry Society.

LUCY HAMILTON lives in Hythe, Kent. "I started secondary school teaching in Whitechapel and Brixton in 1973 and ended a 20 year teaching career in Cambridge. During these years my chief writing outlet was a journal in which I recorded thoughts, feelings, observations and notes about current reading. This constituted a kind of lifeline. I moved to Kent in 1996 and joined The Poetry School in 1997. My fiction and reviews have been published in *Quality Women's Fiction* and poetry in *Staple New Writing, Smiths Knoll* and *The Interpreter's House*." She is included in the anthology, *Parents* (Enitharmon Press, 2000).

DIANA HENDRY Her first collection, *Making Blue* (Peterloo Poets, 1995) was described by Charles Tomlinson as possessing "energy, variety, enviable wit and invention". A second collection from Peterloo, *Borderers*, was published 2001. She has also published a collection of poems for children, *Strange Goings-On* (Viking, 1995). Diana has written more than 30 books for children. Her junior novel, *Harvey Angell* won a Whitbread Award. Her poetry has appeared in many magazines and won several prizes, including first prize in the Housman Poetry Society Competition. She also writes adult short stories, a number of which have been broadcast on Radio 4.

PHOEBE HESKETH lives in Heath Charnock in Lancashire. The daughter of the pioneer radiologist A.E. Rayner, she was born in Preston in 1909 and educated at Cheltenham Ladies College. During WW2 she worked for the *Bolton Evening News* and was later a free-lance lecturer, poetry teacher and journalist, also producing scripts for the BBC. She began writing poetry at an early age but her first book was not published until 1939. It was followed by eleven further volumes before her *Collected Poems, Netting the Sun* were published by Enitharmon in 1989. Since then, three later book of poems have been published by Enitharmon, *Sundowner, The Leave Train* and *A Box of Silver Birch*. Her poetry for younger readers has been published in *Song of Sunlight*, 1974 and *Six of the Best* (Puffin, 1989).

SELIMA HILL has 7 poetry collections. The two latest are *Violet* and *Bunny* (Bloodaxe, 1997 and 2001). She was the only poet to be shortlisted for the Forward, T S Eliot and Whitbread Prizes in 1999 and was T S Eliot prize judge in 2000. *Bunny* was awarded the 2002 Whitbread Prize. Her next collection will be *Portrait of My Lover as a Horse*, also from Bloodaxe.

LIZ HOUGHTON lives in London. "My writing focusses on the fine detail of relationships - between the generations, between siblings, and between the sexes. I was born in 1945. I have a degree in Social Sciences from Birmingham University and studied English Literature at Sydney University. I worked in journalism for 27 years, mainly on national newspapers. Six years ago I gave up to concentrate on creative writing, poetry and novels." Her poetry has appeared in magazines and anthologies, including *The Long Pale Corridor, Contemporary Poems of Bereavement* (Bloodaxe, 1996) and *Parents* (Enitharmon Books, 2000).

SUE HUBBARD is the founder member of Blue Nose Poets which runs workshops and events in London and residential courses at the Abbey in Sutton Courtney, Oxford. She did not start writing seriously until her late 30s. She now works as an art critic (writes regularly for the *Independent on Sunday*) broadcaster, novelist, award-winning poet and Arvon Tutor. She held the Poetry Society's first Residency as Public Art Poet. Her IMAX poem at Waterloo is London's largest public poem. Her first collection was *Everything Begins with the Skin* (Enitharmon Press, 1994), her first novel *Depth of Field* (Dewi Lewis Publishing, 2000). She is included in the anthology, *Oxford Poets 2000*, from Carcanet.

ELIZABETH JENNINGS, who was born in Lincolnshire in 1926 and spent most of her life in Oxford, sadly died while this anthology was in preparation. She had seventeen collections of poetry published, beginning in 1953 with *Poems* and her choice from all these was included in *Collected Poems*, published by Carcanet in 1986. This includes translations and poems for children. In the Preface to *Collected Poems* she says, "Art is not self-expression, while, for me, 'confessional poetry' is almost a contradiction in terms." Anne Stevenson has written of her work, "Hers is a rare, enlightened, classical - and extremely tough - sensibility . . . *Collected Poems* not only represents Elizabeth Jennings at her best, but contains some of the finest lyric poetry of the 20th century."

SYLVIA KANTARIS Poet and critic, she lives in Helston, Cornwall. She has published 7 collections of poems, most recently *Dirty Washing: New and Selected Poems* (Bloodaxe, 1989) and *Lad's Love* (Bloodaxe, 1993). She has also published two collaborations, *News from the Front* with D M Thomas (Arc, 1983) and *The Air Mines of Mistila* with Philip Gross (Bloodaxe, 1988).

MARTHA KAPOS is an American living in London. "After a degree in classics at Harvard, I came to London to study at the Chelsea College of Art where I now teach. Reading, particularly contemporary American poets and French symbolist poets, had been very important to me before I even dreamt of writing myself. I started writing about ten years ago, and since then poetry has become the focus of my life." In 1989, The Many Press brought out a pamphlet and poems have been published in a number of magazines, including *Agenda, Rialto, Poetry London, Thumbscrew* and the *TLS*. She was one of 11 poets included in the first anthology from The Poetry School, *Tying the Song* (Enitharmon Press, 2000), and was short-listed for the *Poetry Review* Dearmer Prize in 2000.

JUDITH KAZANTZIS has published 8 collections of poetry since 1977, including a *Selected Poems 1977-1992*, published in 1995. Her latest two books are *The Odysseus Poems: Fictions On The Odyssey Of Homer* (Cargo, 1999) and *Swimming Through The Grand Hotel* (Enitharmon Press, 1997). Her first novel, *Of Love And Terror*, is due from SAQI Books in 2002. "When my children were growing up in the early seventies, I began to write poetry in earnest. I wanted to touch emotions and argument in a swift heightened conversation, largely in free verse. My poetry has been inextricably personal and political. It started with women, then the pity and anger about how women have had to struggle and men and children with them. But there is no poetry without imagination and the play of feeling and the love of words, and that is the heart of it."

MIMI KHALVATI lives in London working as a free-lance creative writing tutor and Coordinator of The Poetry School which she founded. She started writing in her early 40s after attending an Arvon Foundation course. She has published four full collections with Carcanet, *In White Ink*, 1991, *Mirrorwork*, 1995 for which she received an Arts Council of England Writer's Award, *Entries on Light*, 1997, *The Chine*, 2001. Her *Selected Poems* was published by Carcanet in 2000. She co-edited with Pascale Petit *Tying the Song*, the Poetry School's first anthology (Enitharmon Books, 2000).

LOTTE KRAMER has published 9 collections of poetry. She is published in England, Eire, USA, Canada, and Germany and in many journals and anthologies. She was born in Mainz, Germany and came to England as a refugee child in 1939. She undertook all kinds of work (laundry, dress-shop) while studying Art and History of Art in evening classes. She began writing late in the Seventies, facing up to childhood memories and loss. She felt isolated and writing released trauma. Her latest collections are: *The Phantom Lane* (Rockingham Press, 2000), *Selected and New Poems 1980-1997* (Rockingham Press, 1997). In 1999, a bilingual edition of *Selected Poems* was published in Germany where she now give readings.

GWYNETH LEWIS writes in Welsh and English. She won a Gregory Award in 1988 and published collections in Welsh in 1990, 1996, and 1999. Her first collection in English, *Parables & Faxes* (Bloodaxe, 1994) was shortlisted for the Forward Prize for Best First Collection and won the Aldeburgh Poetry Festival Prize. Her latest collection is *Zero Gravity* (Bloodaxe, 1998) a Poetry Book Society Recommendation. Born in Cardiff, she studied English at Cambridge and in America as a Harkness Fellow. She was recently awarded a NESTA Fellowship and in 2002 published her first book of prose, *Sunbathing in the Rain*.

DINAH LIVINGSTONE lives in London. Recent collections are: *Time on Earth - Selected and New Poems* (Rockingham Press, 1999), *May Day* (Katabasis, 1997). She ran the Camden Voices poetry group from 1978-1998 and her *Poetry Handbook for Readers and Writers* (MacMillan, 1992) is dedicated to them. She translates Latin American poetry and prose, including most recently *Nosotras: Poems by Nicaraguan Women* (NSC, London, 1999) and *Zapatista Stories* by Subcomandante Marcos (Katabasis, 2001). She runs the small press, Katabasis, and her recent prose book, *The Poetry of Earth*, is an essay on poetry, language, theology, ecology and politics, attempting a down-to-earth ('katabasic') poetic.

MAIRI MACINNES was born and brought up in England but spent a large proportion of her adult life abroad, principally in the USA, where she is widely published. She returned to England some ten years ago and now lives in York. Her most recent poetry collections are *The Pebble* (University of Illinois, 2000) and *The Ghostwriter* (Bloodaxe Books, 2000). Previous publications include, *Elsewhere and Back* (Bloodaxe, 1993) and *Herring, Oatmeal, Milk and Salt* (Quarterly Review of Literature Series, 1984).

KATHLEEN McPHILEMY was born in Northern Ireland and since lived in Edinburgh, London and Oxford. She works in Further Education. Her latest collection is *A Tented Peace* (Katabasis, 1995).

MARY MACRAE has lived in London all her life. "Poetry came to me as a sudden revelation, hearing Masefield's *Cargoes* read on the wireless when I was a small child. I've read poetry ever since and written it sporadically. My working life has been spent teaching English, but four years ago I decided that, as far as writing went, it was now or never. I discovered the Poetry School and Second Light Network and, soon after, took early retirement. Since then, I've been published in various magazines and am also one of the editors of *Magma* poetry magazine."

SARAH MAGUIRE was born in West London where she has lived all her life. Her collections are *Spilt Milk* and *The Invisible Mender* (Cape Poetry, 1997) which included a translation of Marina Tsvetaeva's 'Wires'. She is a frequent contributor to Kaleidescope and other BBC Radio arts programmmes. In 1996 she was awarded a Bursary by the Arts Council of Great Britain.

BARBARA MARSH "I'm a singer/song-writer/musician, so music and especially words have always had a strong pull on me. It has only been in the last two years that my poetry has felt 'right' to me as if some sudden shift has occurred. I am an American and have lived in London for over 17 years and I think cross-cultural reference adds an angle to my work." Her work was included in the anthology, *Parents*, published by Enitharmon, 2000.

GERDA MAYER was born in Karlsbad, Czechoslovakia and came to England in 1939 at the age of 11. Among her collections of poetry are a shared one with Elon and Halpern, *Treble Poets 2* and *The Knockabout Show*, both from Chatto and Windus; *Monkey on the Analyst's Couch*, Ceolfrith Press, which was a Poetry Book Society Recommendation; *A Heartache of Grass*, Peterloo Poets. Her latest collection is *Bernini's Cat*, Iron Press, 1999.

ELMA MITCHELL sadly died during the preparation of this anthology. She was born in Airdrie, Scotland in 1919, worked in London for many years and latterly lived and worked in Somerset as a free-lance writer and translator. She was a professional librarian. Four poetry collections have been published by Peterloo Poets: *The Poor Man in the Flesh*, 1976; *The Human Cage*, 1979; *Furnished Rooms*, 1983; *People Etcetera*, 1987, which included the best poems from the two earliest collections (now out-of-print) and new poems. She was first prize winner in the Cheltenham Festival Poetry Competition in 1977.

LYN MOIR was born in Glasgow in 1934. Her childhood was divided between Scotland and the USA, where her poems were published in 1952. After a busy family and professional life, she began writing seriously again in 1988 and since 1990 has been published widely in poetry magazines. A first collection, *Me and Galileo*, was published by Arrowhead Press in 2001. She regularly acts as guest editor for the Second Light Network Newsletter.

FELICITY NAPIER lives in Twickenham where she teaches writing groups in mental health settings. "I have been writing poetry, short fiction and drama for 20 years, poetry remaining my first love. My poems have won prizes and have appeared in numerous magazines and anthologies and been broadcast on radio and TV. A selection of my work appeared in *Anvil New Poets*, 1990. The writing process is an integral part of my life, my touchstone and survival route."

CAROLINE NATZLER "Writing has always been important . . . The impulse has shifted from a young desire to voice my inner self to a commitment to writing as a lesbian, and latterly to a pleasure in the craft . . . Although I wrote poetry in my teens I came to think of it as too difficult or esoteric and did not start again until I was 40 . . . " Her short-story collection, *Water Wings*, was published by Onlywomen Press in 1990. A poetry pamphlet, *Speaking the Wetlands* (Pikestaff Press, 1998) was followed by a full collection, *Design Fault* (Flambard Press, 2001). She has now given up part-time work as a lawyer to concentrate on her writing and on teaching creative writing.

DOROTHY NIMMO Until her death in 2001, which sadly took place while this anthology was in preparation, she lived in Settle, North Yorkshire. "I was born in 1932, educated at York and Cambridge and spent 30 years being a wife-and-mother, a gardener and a goat-herd. I started writing in the 1980's in a WEA class, and went on to Arvon courses and an MA in creative writing at Lancaster University, 1989. I left home to be caretaker of the Friends Meeting House in Gloucester and am now caretaker at the Settle Friends Meeting House." She had five collections published. The two latest were *The Children's Game*, 1998, a Poetry Book Society Recommendation, *The Wigbox: New and Selected Poems*, 2000, both from Smith / Doorstop Books. She won a Cholmondely Award in 1997.

RUTH PADEL's fifth poetry collection is *Voodoo Shop* (PBS Recommendation, Chatto and Windus, 2000). She is author of *I'm a Man* (Faber, 2000), a study of Greek myth, rock music and modern masculinity, and invented the *Independent on Sunday's* 'Sunday Poem' column. A selection from it, entitled *52 Ways of Looking At A Poem Or How Modern Poetry Can Change Your Life* is published (Chatto and Windus, 2002). She is a Fellow of the Society of Authors and has won the National Poetry Prize. She lives in London.

EVANGELINE PATERSON sadly died while this Anthology was in preparation. She formerly lived in Jesmond, Newcastle on Tyne. "I started to write in the 1970's when my children were past the dependent stage. I expect I write more about domestic affairs than a man would, but I also write about events in the wider world - the sort of subjects a man might choose, but I think I deal with them from a more personal perspective". Her last collection was *A Game of Soldiers*, Stride 1997. She was one of the Editors of *Other Poetry*.

MEG PEACOCKE was born in 1930. She has written poetry since childhood but began to publish only after she came to live on a Cumbrian hill farm in 1984. Her most recent collection is *Selves* (Peterloo Poets, 1995). She works as a Counsellor, gives readings and runs occasional workshops.

PASCALE PETIT was born in Paris, grew up in France and Wales and has an MA in sculpture from the Royal College of Art. "When I stopped being a visual artist I applied myself wholeheartedly to poetry. The page became my studio where I had to create my world and make it real. Metaphors and images replaced materials: the labour-intensive process of sculpture I now apply to making my poems." Her first collection was *Heart of a Deer* (Enitharmon, 1998), her second, *The Zoo Father* (Seren, 2001) is a PBS Recommendation and was short-listed for the T S Eliot Prize. She was short-listed for the Forward Prize for Best Single Poem in 2000, has travelled extensively in the Venezuelan Amazon and is Poetry Editor of *Poetry London*. With Mimi Khalvati, she edited the first anthology of the Poetry School, *Tying the Song* (Enitharmon, 2000).

PATRICIA POGSON lives near Kendal in Cumbria. "I started writing in my early 30s when my children started school. I was encouraged by early publication and have since produced 5 collections". Publications include, *Rattling the Handle* (Littlewood, 1990). Her latest, *The Tides in the Basin* (Flambard Press,1994), will be followed by *Holding*, dedicated to her late husband, the poet Geoffrey Holloway, published by Flambard Books in 2002.

PEGGY POOLE was born and brought up in Kent, and has lived in Wirral for many years. Her poetry publications include the collections *Hesitations* (Brentham, 1990), *Trusting the Rainbow* (Brentham, 1994), *From the Tide's Edge* (1999) and a recent pamphlet, *Polishing Pans* (Driftwood, 2001). She has also edited several anthologies, including *Marigolds Grow Wild on Platforms* (Cassell, 1996), and writes poetry for children. A contributor to *Writer's News* and *Writing*, she was formerly a poetry consultant for BBC Radio North West's 'Write Now'.

JOAN POULSON lives in Manchester. She has poems in around three hundred anthologies for adults and children internationally and her poetry has been used extensively by Radio 4. She has won prizes in USA, Canada and this country. Her pamphlet, *earth being*, was published by Flarestack, 2000, followed by a poetry collection, *onetree* (Blackthorn, 2001). Her novel, *Dear Ms*, was published by A&C Black, 2001.

CAROLINE PRICE Violinist and teacher living and working in Kent. Her poems and stories have won prizes and have appeared widely in magazines and anthologies. "I started writing prose as a child and added poetry in my 20s. Writing for me lives hand in hand with music and has always been an essential and unquestioned part of my life". Her second collection of poetry was *Pictures Against Skin* (Rockingham Press, 1994). In 1997 she was one of ten poets involved in a Women Writers' Exchange, taking part in readings and discussions in England and Northern Europe.

KATHLEEN RAINE has published 11 volumes of poetry and also prose works, including *Golgonooza, City of the Imagination (Last Studies of William Blake).* Her *Collected Poems* appeared in 1981. Her *Selected Poems* was published by Golgonooza Press in 1988 and a re-issued long poem, *On A Deserted Shore*, by Agenda Editions, 1995.

IRENE RAWNSLEY lives in North Yorkshire where she writes poems and stories and is a creative writing tutor for the Open College of the Arts. Her most recent collection is *Hiding Out* (Smith / Doorstop Books, 1996).

MICHÈLE ROBERTS is half-French, half-English and has homes in both countries. She is a novelist whose novel *Daughters of the House* (Virago, 1992) was short-listed for the Booker Prize and won the W H Smith Literary Award. She has been poetry editor of *Spare Rib* and *City Limits* and her poetry has been widely published in magazines and anthologies. Her collections include *The Mirror of the Mother* (1986), *Psyche and the Hurricane* (1990) and *All the Selves I Was* (Virago Poetry, 1995). She is Professor of Creative Writing at the University of East Anglia.

ANNE RYLAND was born in 1962 in Essex. She lived for a number of years in London, teaching German in schools, and then moved to Northumberland, where landscape and coastline inspire her writing. She has had poems published in a range of magazines, including *Acumen, Smiths Knoll, Other Poetry, Envoi* and *Seam* and is now studying for an MA in Writing Poetry at Newcastle University. She works as a tutor of Adult Basic Education at her local community centre.

JULIE SAMPSON lives in Devon. She is a visiting lecturer at the University of the West of England and works as part-time visiting lecturer and tutor of Creative Writing at various local colleges. She has researched and published articles on the poet HD (Hilda Doolittle) and is now working on a book and a sequence of poems about women writers from Devon, from the 15th to the 20th century. She has had poems published in a variety of magazines and she was runner-up for the Exeter Poetry prize in 1999.

ANN SANSOM has a pamphlet and two books published under the name of Ann Dancy. Her first full-length collection as Ann Sansom, *Romance*, was published by Bloodaxe in 1994. *Vehicle* was published by Slow Dancer Press in 1999.

CAROLE SATYAMURTI lives and works in London as poet and sociologist, teaching at the University of East London and at the Tavistock Clinic. "I am principally interested in the relevance of psychoanalytic ideas to the stories people tell about themselves, whether in formal autobiography or in everyday encounters." She won the National Poetry Competition in 1986, was awarded an Art's Council Writers' Award in 1988. She has published *Broken Moon*, 1987, *Changing the Subject*, 1990, *Striking Distance*, 1994, all from OUP, together with *Selected Poems*, 1998. *Love and Variations* was issued in 2000. She has given many readings and is an experienced workshop tutor - with Gregory Warren Wilson, she recently conducted a series of workshops on Art and Poetry at the National Gallery. She received a Chomondeley Award in 2000.

MYRA SCHNEIDER "Writing has been essential to my well-being since I was nine. In the early 1960s I found the poetry scene unsympathetic, so concentrated on writing prose and I had novels published for children and teenagers. In my forties I started writing poetry again. I write to explore my own life and the lives of others. I love using narrative in poetry. Perhaps the keynote of my work is finding a voice." Most recent collections are, *The Panic Bird* and *Insisting on Yellow, New and Selected Poems*, both Enitharmon Press, 1998 and 2000. Her writing handbook, written with poet John Killick, is *Writing for Self-Discovery* (Vega, Chrysalis Books, 2002). She recently edited, with Dilys Wood, an anthology, *Parents*, (Enitharmon Books / Second Light, 2000). *Writing My Way Through Cancer*, will be published by Jessica Kingsley in Spring 2003.

RUTH SHARMAN lives in London with her husband and young son. She has been widely published in magazines and anthologies and her poetry prizes include second in the 1989 Arvon Competition. "My first collection, *Birth of the Owl Butterflies* (Picador, 1997) was published in the year that our first child was born. I had come late to motherhood and it had taken ten years for the book of poems to mature. At six I was uprooted from southern India. The sense of dislocation continued. I wore academic achievements as a kind of mask and disconnection from my inner world led to constant illness. My mother died just as I was finishing a Ph.D. at Cambridge and it was then through writing and psychoanalysis that I began to obtain a sense of identity. For me, poetry comes out of an intense preoccupation with time passing. It is through poetry that I feel most intensely alive."

PENELOPE SHUTTLE lives in Cornwall with her husband, the poet, Peter Redgrove. Her seventh collection, *A Leaf Out Of His Book* appeared in 1999 from Oxford Poets / Carcanet. She is currently working on a new collection, provisionally entitled, *The Tattooist Re-Opens Her Parlour*. She has a grown-up daughter, Zoe.

HYLDA SIMS divides her time between Ipswich and London and runs Saturday evening Poetry and Jazz at the Poetry Cafe in Covent Garden, London. She writes fiction, poetry and songs. Her novel, *Inspecting the Island*, based on A S Neill's controversial school, Summerhill, where she was a pupil, was published in 2001. *Reaching Peckham*, a narrative sequence of poems, has been set to music and performed at Festivals and on the London fringe.

RUTH SMITH lives in Bromley in Kent. "I've written poetry for five years and found nothing to equal the excitement. Having spent a career as an English teacher passing judgment on children's writing I began to appreciate the difficulties and admire their talent. I had read little contemporary poetry and, after first managing my writing on my own with many failures and a few poems published, I found that a poetry workshop at Morley College helped tremendously." She won the London Writers' Prize in 1996 and two of her poems appeared in the first edition of Faber and Faber's *First Pressings*.

MARGARET SPEAK lives in York. "I began writing in my late 30s in response to the death of my younger sister. I was encouraged by early success in competitions and being a featured poet in *Giant Steps*. Since then I've also had prizes with short stories and gained a Master's degree in writing. Exploring ideas and images in words helps me make sense of emotional experience and allows me to re-tell stories which reflect women's issues through changing social conditions." She has a collection, *The Firefly Cage* (Redbeck Press, 1998).

PAULINE STAINER has five collections published with Bloodaxe. Her fourth, *The Wound-dresser's Dream*, was shortlisted for the Whitbread Prize. Her most recent collection, *Parable Island*, was written on a three-year stay in Orkney. *The Lady and the Hare, New and Selected Poems* is due from Bloodaxe in 2003.

ANNE STEVENSON is an American poet long resident in Britain. She has had ten collections of poetry published by the Oxford University Press. After the collapse of OUP Poetry in 1998, she contracted with Bloodaxe Books. *Granny Scarecrow* appeared in May 2000 and was shortlisted for both the T S Eliot and the Whitbread prizes.

ALICIA STUBBERSFIELD was born in St Helen's, Lancashire and taught English in a large comprensive in Stockport for fifteen years. She lived for some years in Yorkshire where she won the Yorkshire Open Poetry Competition in 1991,1992 and 1993. In 1992 she gained an MA in Creative Writing from Lancaster University which she followed with research into the American feminist poet and novelist, Marge Piercy. Her collection *The Magician's Assistant* was published by Flambard in 1994 and *Unsuitable Shoes* by the Collective Press in 1999. She now lives in Wales, working as tutor for the Open College of the Arts and freelancing as a writer.

ISOBEL THRILLING lives in Romford in Essex. She was born in Suffolk, raised in a mining village in Yorkshire, went to Hull University and for many years was Head of an English Language Service in London. "I first started writing after eye-operations which saved my sight. My work is very visual and perhaps, subconsciously, I am creating aural images. Poetry has made me aware of childhood traumas, which previously I had no way to express. I explore silences and what lies behind appearance. Women bring a different focus to words. Poetry is the writer's ectoplasm, a precipitation of the imagination, a leap across the synapses of the brain". Her most recent collections are *Spectrum Shift* (Littlewood, 1991) and *The Chemistry of Angels* (halfacrown press, 2000).

VAL WARNER lives in London. She received a Gregory Award for Poetry and has been Writer-in-Residence at University College, Swansea and Dundee University. She runs Harrow Writers' Workshop. She has published three poetry collections with Carcanet, including *Tooting Idyll* (1998) and *The Centenary Corbiere* (translation), and edited Charlotte Mew's *Selected* (Carcanet, 1997) and, earlier, *the Collected*. With Anne Harvey, she performs a dramatic presentation of Mew's work. Short stories in *Edinburgh Review, Encounter, The London Magazine, PEN New Fiction (Quartet)* and other journals.

SUSAN WICKS is the author of 3 collections of poetry. "I've almost always written but didn't manage to get a book accepted until my early 40s . . . The most telling difficulty was lack of self-confidence . . . There were few models. I'm from a relatively unbookish background. I wrote prose fiction in my teens and early 20s - it didn't strike me that poetry was something a woman might write". Her most recent collection, *The Clever Daughter* (Faber and Faber, 1997) was a Poetry Book Society Choice and short-listed for both the T S Eliot and Forward Prizes. Her first, *Singing Underwater* (1992) won the Aldeburgh Poetry Festival Prize. She has also published a short memoir, *Driving My Father*, and 2 novels. She has recently been appointed Lecturer in Creative Writing at the University of Kent, in Canterbury. She lives in West Kent with her husband and younger daughter.

MERRYN WILLIAMS lives in Wootton, in Bedfordshire. "I gave up writing poems at university and only took it up again when my younger children started at school". Her latest collection of poems is *The Latin Master's Story*, Rockingham Press, 2000. She is editor of *The Interpreter's House* poetry magazine and edits the newsletter of the Wilfred Owen Association.

FRANCES WILSON lives in Ware, Hertfordshire. "Writing has always shared space in my working life with teaching and illustrating. I wrote short stories until 1986 when I started writing poems. I have won prizes in various poetry competitions. My pamphlet, *Where the Light Gets In* was published by Poet and Printer, 1992 and collection, *Close to Home* by Rockingham in 1993. I will shortly complete a second collection".

DILYS WOOD had a Welsh father and was brought up in South Wales. She now lives in London. She served in the Cabinet Office as Secretary of the Women's National Commission, which re-vitalised her interest in women's matters. In her 50s she founded the Second Light Network (SLN), which helps older women poets make contacts with others and develops, supports and publishes their work. She edits SLN's Newsletter. She co-edited, with Myra Schneider, the anthology *Parents* (Enitharmon, 2000) joining in country-wide readings. Through SLN, Dilys aims to publicise that women not only form the back-bone of the poetry writing- reading- and book-buying public, but often write more deeply, imaginatively and adventurously as they gain age, confidence and perspective. Her collection, *Women Come to a Death*, was published by Katabasis, 1997.

LYNNE WYCHERLEY lives in Kidlington, Oxfordshire. "Born on the edge of the Fens in 1962, I began writing in 1996. I have worked in nature conservation, archeology and second-hand books. I am particularly drawn to poetry that explores spiritual roots, love and the environment. I appreciate the work of many mature women poets and do not regret being a slightly late starter - I'm glad to have seen different aspects of life, love, grief before beginning writing." Her poems have won several competitions. Her pamphlets are *Cracks in the Ice* (Acumen Publications, 1999) and *A Sea of Dark Fields* (Hilton House, 2000). She was Blue Nose Poet of the Year in 1998.

ACKNOWLEDGEMENTS

Thanks are due to the following copyright holders for permission to publish the poems in this anthology:

Anna Adams and Enitharmon Press for 'The Self Portrait', 'Black-House Woman', 'Tortoiseshells Overwintering', 'At Mauthausen Camp'; from *Green Resistance* (1996): (c) Anna Adams

Fleur Adcock and Bloodaxe Books Ltd for 'Script', 'Kilpeck', 'Letter from Highgate Wood' from *Poems* 1960-2000 (2001): (c) Fleur Adcock

Gillian Allnutt and Bloodaxe Books Ltd for 'The Garden in Esh Winning', 'What You Need to Know for Praying', 'Gone' from *Nantucket and the Angel* (1997): (c) Gillian Allnutt

Moniza Alvi and Bloodaxe Books Ltd. for 'And If' from *Carrying My Wife* (2001); and 'The Twins': (c) Moniza Alvi

R.V. Bailey for 'The Greyhound': (c) R.V.Bailey

Jill Bamber and the National Poetry Foundation for 'Windmill': (c) Jill Bamber

Wendy Bardsley and Headland Publications for 'October Apples', 'Maya Ceramic Figure' and 'Pebbles' from *Steel Wings* (1998): (c) Wendy Bardsley

Wanda Barford and Flambard Press for 'Beetroot' from *Sweet Wine & Bitter Herbs* (1996 and 1999): (c) Wanda Barford

Elizabeth Bartlett and Bloodaxe Books Ltd. for 'Lamb', 'A Nodal Point, 'The Beautiful Knees of the Visiting Lay Preacher' from *Two Women Dancing: New and Selected Poems* (1995); and Headland Publications for 'Irish Hair' from *Instead of a Mass* (1991): (c) Elizabeth Bartlett

Jacqueline Bartlett for 'Mummies : (c) Jacqueline Bartlett

Jane Beeson and Headland Publications for 'Star-eyed Fool' and 'Arthritis' from *Quartz* (1997): (c) Jane Beeson

Anne Beresford and Katabasis for 'What Do You Do All Day When I'm at School?' from *No Place for Cowards* (1998); and Agenda Editions and Bellow Publishing for 'Home Visit' from *Selected and New Poems* (1997)

Elizabeth Bewick and Peterloo Poets for 'Heartsease' from *Heartsease* (1991): (c) Elizabeth Bewick

Patricia Bishop and Oversteps Books for 'Parabolas' from *Saving Dragons* (2000): (c) Patricia Bishop

Anne Born and Headland Publications for 'Hooks' from *Lighting Effects* (1987); and Headland Publications for 'A Dog's Life in Bosnia' from *Planting Light* (1999): (c) Anne Born

Pat Borthwick and Pharos Press for 'The Scan' (2000): (c) Pat Borthwick

Jacqueline Brown and Littlewood Arc for 'In the Room II', 'Poaching', 'Finality of Egg' from *Thinking Egg* (1993): (c) Jacqueline Brown

Nadine Brummer and Shoestring Press for 'Hazel Nuts', 'At the Lucian Freud Exhibition' from *A Question of Blue Tulips* (1999): (c) Nadine Brummer

Catherine Byron and Loxwood Stoneleigh for 'Silk and Belfast Linen' (I, II and III), 'Fat Hen' from *The Fat-Hen Field Hospital Poems 1985-1992* (1993): (c) Catherine Byron

Sally Carr and Rockingham Press for 'Soft Fruit' from *Electrons on Bonfire Night* (1997): (c) Sally Carr

Liz Cashdan and Five Leaves Publications for 'The Wool Trade' from *Laughing All The Way* (1995): (c) Liz Cashdan

Alison Chisholm and Headland Publications for 'Swimming with Dolphins' from *Daring the Slipstream* (1997): (c) Alison Chisholm

Gillian Clarke and Carcanet Press Ltd for 'Miracle on St David's Day' from *Collected Poems* (1997); and 'Ark', "The Field Mouse', 'At the Glass Factory' and 'Her Table' from 'Glass', from *Five Fields* (1998): (c) Gillian Clarke

Anne Cluysenaar and Carcanet Press Ltd for '10' and '16' from 'Vaughan Variations ' from *Timeslips, New and Selected Poems* (1997); and 'Stilled': (c) Anne Cluysenaar

Gladys Mary Coles and Duckworth & Co. Ltd for 'The Glass Island', 'Late August Fireworks, Llandudno Bay' from *The Glass Island* (1992 and 1994); and 'After Edgehill, 1642', 'Leafburners' from *Leafburners: New and Selected Poems* (1986): (c) Gladys Mary Coles

Wendy Cope and Faber & Faber Ltd for 'By the Round Pond' from *If I Don't Know* (2001); 'The Lavatory Attendant' from *Making Cocoa for Kingsley Amis* (1986); and Headland Publications for 'Les Vacances' from *The Poet's View* ed Gladys Mary Coles 1996: (c) Wendy Cope

Elsa Corbluth and Peterloo Poets for 'Dirge for St Patrick's Night' from *St Patrick's Night* (1985): (c) Elsa Corbluth

Tricia Corob for 'Afternoons' from 'India Notebook': (c) Tricia Corob

Hilary Davies and Enitharmon Press for 'Autumn' from 'When the Animals Come', *In a Valley of this Restless Mind* (1997) : (c) Hilary Davies

Angela Dove for 'Caroline Crachami's Skeleton': (c) Angela Dove

Jane Duran and Enitharmon Press for 'Forty Eight', 'The Orange Tree in Cordoba', from *Breathe Now, Breathe* (1995); 'Maestrazgo' and 'Battle of Teruel, Winter 1937-8', from *Silences from the Spanish Civil War* (2002): (c) Jane Duran

Jean Earle the Estate of Jean Earle and Seren Books for 'Two Rhondda Valley Poems', 'The Fox', 'Stillborn' from *Selected Poems* (1990): (c) the Estate of Jean Earle

Christine Evans for 'Bluebells from Nanhoron' : (c) Christine Evans

Ruth Fainlight and Hutchinson for 'The Lace-wing' from *Another Full Moon* (1976) and 'Aeneas' Meeting with the Sibyl' from *Sibyls and Others* (1980): (c) Ruth Fainlight

U.A. Fanthorpe and Peterloo Poets for 'Kinch & Lack' from *Consequences* (2000); 'Resuscitation Team' and 'Janus' from *Standing To* (1982), 'What about Jerusalem?': (c) U.A. Fanthorpe

Elaine Feinstein and Carcanet Press Ltd for 'Against Winter', 'Getting Older' and 'Home' from *Selected Poems* (1994); and 'Living Room' from *Gold* (2000): (c) Elaine Feinstein

Kate Foley and Blackwater Press for 'Tall Foreign Doctor', 'Fox on the Stairs', 'Here's the House, where's the Steeple?', 'The Only Ghost' from *A Year without Apricots* (1999): (c) Kate Foley

Wendy French for 'On the Sunny Side' : (c) Wendy French

Katherine Frost for 'Our Son Has Two Mothers' : (c) Katherine Frost

Cynthia Fuller and Flambard Press for 'Dream Fish' from *Only a Small Boat* (2001) : (c) Cynthia Fuller

Anne-Marie Fyfe and Rockingham Press for 'Our House' from *Tickets from a Blank Window* (2002): (c) Anne-Marie Fyfe

Katherine Gallagher and Arc Publications for 'Poem for a Shallot', 'Hunger', 'Jet Lag', 'A Visit to the War Memorial, Canberra' from *Tigers on the Silk Road* (2000) : (c) Katherine Gallagher

Pamela Gillilan the Estate of Pamela Gillilan and Bloodaxe Books Ltd for 'Country Living, 1955', 'August' from *The Rashomon Syndrome* (1998) : (c) the Estate of Pamela Gillilan

Ann Gray and Headland Publications for 'Solace' from *The Man I Was Promised* (2003) : (c) Ann Gray

Cathy Grindrod and Headland Publications for 'Dispossessed' from *Fighting Talk* (2003): Cathy Grindrod

Lucy Hamilton for 'Rings' : (c) Lucy Hamilton

Diana Hendry and Peterloo Poets for 'In Defence of Pianos', 'The Lace Makers' from *Making Blue* (1995) : (c) Diana Hendry

Phoebe Hesketh and Enitharmon Press for 'Mary', 'Gone Away', 'Preparing to Leave', 'After Ecclesiastes' from *The Leave Train: New and Selected Poems* (1994): (c) Phoebe Hesketh

Selima Hill and Bloodaxe Books Ltd for 'I am Hers and she is Mine', 'The Fish Hospital' from *Violet* (1997): (c) Selima Hill

Liz Houghton for 'Persian Lamb': (c) Liz Houghton

Sue Hubbard and Enitharmon Press for 'Assimilation' from *Everything Begins with the Skin* (1994): (c) Sue Hubbard

Elizabeth Jennings David Higham Associates and Carcanet Press Ltd for 'Tribute', 'Song for a Birth or a Death', 'The Island'. 'Song at the Beginning of Autumn' from *Collected Poems* (1986) : (c) David Higham Associates

Sylvia Kantaris and Bloodaxe Books Ltd for 'Some Untidy Spot', 'O Little Star' from *Dirty Washing, New and Selected Poems* (1989): (c) Sylvia Kantaris

Martha Kapos for 'Fishing in an Old Wound', 'Origin of the Sexes According to Aristophanes' : (c) Martha Kapos

Judith Kazantzis and Enitharmon Press for 'A Photograph Seen When I Was Twelve,. 'For Mahesh, Deported' from *Swimming Through the Grand Hotel* (1997): (c) Judith Kazantzis

Mimi Khalvati and Carcanet Press Ltd for 'The Piano', 'Villanelle', 'Middle Age', 'Writing Letters' from *The Chine* (2002); and a section from 'Entries on Light' from *Entries on Light* (1997) : (c) Mimi Khalvati

Lotte Kramer and Rockingham Press for 'Earthquake', 'Cocoon', 'Bilingual' from *Selected and New Poems, 1980-1997* (1997) : (c) Lotte Kramer

Gwyneth Lewis and Bloodaxe Books Ltd for 'Coconut Postcards', 'Stone Walls' from *Zero Gravity* (1998): (c) Gwyneth Lewis

Dinah Livingstone and Katabasis for 'Maytime', 'This', 'The Excluded' from *May Day* (1997) : (c) Dinah Livingstone

Mairi MacInnes and Bloodaxe Books Ltd for 'Mass' from *Elsewhere and Back* (1993) : (c) Mairi MacInnes

Kathleen McPhilemy and Hearing Eye for 'Housewife', 'Birth of a Child' from *'Witness to Magic* (1990): (c) Kathleen McPhilemy

Carole Satyamurti and Oxford University Press Ltd and Bloodaxe Books Ltd for 'from Between the Lines: I', 'Intensive Care', 'Ourstory', 'Woman Bathing in a Stream' from *Selected Poems* (1998) : (c) Carole Satyamurti

Myra Schneider and Enitharmon Press for 'A Letter to Sujata in Bremen', 'The Red Cupboard' and 'Leave Taking' from *Insisting on Yellow* (2000); and 'Flood' : (c) Myra Schneider

Ruth Sharman and Picador for 'The Travancore Evening Brown' from *Birth of the Owl Butterflies* (1997) : (c) Ruth Sharman

Penelope Shuttle, Carcanet Press Ltd and Oxford University Press Ltd for 'My Son', 'Indoors' from *A Leaf Out Of His Book* (1999); and for 'Jungian Cows' from *Selected Poems* (1998) : (c) Penelope Shuttle

Hylda Sims for 'Gulf': (c) Hylda Sims

Ruth Smith for 'Close Quarters': (c) Ruth Smith

Margaret Speak and Redbeck Press for 'Lepus Timidus' from *The Firefly Cage* (1998) : (c) Margaret Speak

Pauline Stainer and Bloodaxe Books Ltd for 'The Plaster Room', 'The Divining of Wounds' from *Honeycomb* (1989); and 'Scarecrow', 'Walking the Tide-line on Ash Wednesday' (c) Pauline Stainer

Anne Stevenson and Bloodaxe Books Ltd for 'An Angel', 'Leaving', 'The White Room' from Granny Scarecrow (2002); 'Four and a Half Dancing Men' from *Four and a Half Dancing Men* (1993); and 'In the Tunnel of Summers' from *Selected Poems* (1987): (c) Anne Stevenson

Alicia Stubbersfield and The Collective Press for 'Human Cannon-Ball' from *Unsuitable Shoes* (1999): (c) Alicia Stubbersfield

Isobel Thrilling and halfacrown Press for 'Bending the Light', 'Blood-Head' from *The Chemistry of Angels* (2000); and Littlewood Arc for 'The Miner' and 'On Blindness' from *Spectrum Shift* (1991) : (c) Isobel Thrilling

Val Warner and Carcanet Press Ltd for 'Dust' from 'Tooting Idyll', from *Tooting Idyll* (1998) : (c) Val Warner

Susan Wicks and Faber & Faber Ltd for 'Persephone', 'Monet :The Chicago Haystacks' from *The Clever Daughter* (1996) : (c) Susan Wicks

Merryn Williams and Rockingham Press for 'Blood Donor', 'Wilfred's Bridge' from *The Latin Master's Story* (2000): (c) Merryn Williams

Frances Wilson and Rockingham Press for 'Making Poppy Dolls', 'Coming of Age', 'Understanding Rodin' from *Close to Home* (1993): (c) Frances Wilson

Dilys Wood for 'Horace's Seventh Ode', 'Friday Fish Man': (c) Dilys Wood

Lynne Wycherley for 'Tawny Owl' : (c) Lynne Wycherley

Headland Publications apologises for any errors or omissions in the above list and would be grateful to be notified of any corrections that should be incorporated in any reprinting of this anthology.